The Measurement
of Economic Welfare

ITS APPLICATION TO THE AGED POOR

Institute for Research on Poverty
Monograph Series

The Measurement of Economic Welfare

ITS APPLICATION TO THE AGED POOR

Marilyn Moon

University of Wisconsin—Madison

ACADEMIC PRESS New York San Francisco London

A Subsidiary of Harcourt Brace Jovanovich, Publishers

This book is one of a series sponsored by the Institute for
Research on Poverty of the University of Wisconsin pursuant to
the provisions of the Economic Opportunity Act of 1964.

ACADEMIC PRESS, INC.
111 Fifth Avenue, New York, New York 10003

United Kingdom Edition published by
ACADEMIC PRESS, INC. (LONDON) LTD.
24/28 Oval Road, London NW1

Library of Congress Cataloging in Publication Data

Moon, Marilyn.
 The measurement of economic welfare.

 (Institute for Research on Poverty monograph series)
 Includes index.
 1.   Aged–United States–Economic conditions.   2.   Old
age assistance–United States.   3.   Aged–Taxation–United
States.   4.   Cost and standard of living–United States.
I.   Title.   II.   Series: Wisconsin.   University–Madison.
Institute for Research on Poverty.   Monograph series.
HQ1064.U5M67   301.43′5   76-50401
ISBN 0–12–504650–2

PRINTED IN THE UNITED STATES OF AMERICA

Contents

List of Tables

List of Figures

Foreword

During the 1960s there was a dramatic increase in research on poverty. But oddly enough very little of it focused on the aged poor. *The Measurement of Economic Welfare: Its Application to the Aged Poor,* is, therefore, a timely addition to both the literature on poverty and the general literature on measurement of economic status.

Moon begins with theoretical considerations of how to measure economic well-being appropriately. She concludes that a measure of potential consumption is superior to the current annual money income measure of economic status. In order to derive an empirical approximation of the potential consumption measure, she makes several adjustments to the annual money income indicator of economic status. These adjustments include an imputation for net worth including home equity; the addition of an estimate of the cash value of three in-kind transfers—Medicare, Medicaid, and public housing; the subtraction of an estimate of income and payroll taxes paid; and the addition of an estimate of intrafamily transfers.

The adjustment for intrafamily transfers is perhaps the most important and innovative. Given the large percentage of the aged who live with their children—30 percent in Moon's 1966 sample—and the even larger percentage that would live with their children if there were no public transfer programs such as Social Security, intrafamily transfers obviously play a very large role in the economic well-being of the aged.

Moon then examines how the rankings of several groups of the aged vary with the definition of economic status that she employs. She discovers, for example, that, relative to the annual money income measure, her more comprehensive measure of economic status places an even larger proportion of families headed by nonwhites in the bottom part of the distribution of economic well-being. An unexpected finding is that more aged families with workers fall into the bottom part of the distribution when the more comprehensive measure of economic status is used.

Finally, Moon employs her more comprehensive definition of economic well-being to examine the impact of government programs on the well-being of the aged. She looks at five cash transfer programs: Social Security, public assistance, government pensions, veterans' benefits, and unemployment insurance and workmen's compensation; three in-kind transfer programs: Medicare, Medicaid, and public housing; and three income tax provisions: the double personal exemption, exclusion of transfer income, and the retirement income tax credit.

The Moon monograph is part of a larger body of Institute work that has been concerned with developing more comprehensive measures of economic status than the current annual money income measure. *Augmenting Economic Measures of Well-Being,* edited by Marilyn Moon and Eugene Smolensky, and *Public Expenditures, Taxes, and the Distribution of Income: The U.S.: 1950, 1961, and 1970,* by Morgan Reynolds and Eugene Smolensky, are the two most recent volumes published in the Institute Monograph Series that deal with this issue. The unique contribution of *The Measurement of Economic Welfare* is its focus on special problems that relate to the aged.

IRWIN GARFINKEL
Director, Institute for Research on Poverty

Preface

This project began with work on my dissertation at the University of Wisconsin—Madison, completed in May 1974. Since then, the manuscript has gone through several revisions while I was employed as a research associate at the Institute for Research on Poverty and as an assistant professor at the University of Wisconsin—Milwaukee. I received research support from the Graduate School of the University of Wisconsin—Madison, the Institute for Research on Poverty, the Social Security Administration, and the Administration on Aging. Competent personnel at the Institute for Research on Poverty eased the burden of this project in several areas. Cathy Ersland, Linda Bielski, and Wendy Haebig skillfully typed several versions. Roberta Kimmel diligently edited the manuscript. I am particularly indebted to Nancy Schofield and Nancy Williamson, whose expert programming assistance greatly enhanced the progress of my research.

Dave Betson, Martin David, and Ron Sepanik commented on parts of the manuscript. Glen Cain, Robert Lampman, and Eugene Smolensky provided particularly cogent advice and direction during the dissertation stage. Michael Taussig was also of substantial aid with his excellent comments on an early draft. As my major professor, Robert Haveman was teacher, critic, and counselor. He encouraged me to complete the manuscript and taught me that research can be exciting. I greatly benefited from the many discussions we had, particularly during the formative stages of the project.

Finally, I wish to thank Douglas Gomery. Although he did not type the manuscript or do more than his share of the housework, he was an invaluable editor and sounding board. His tireless energy in his own work set an example that helped speed this work to completion.

1

The Aged and Economic Welfare

The evaluation of government taxes and expenditures by their distributional consequences has become an increasingly important area of study in the field of public finance. A natural outgrowth of this interest is the search for broader, yet quantifiable measures of economic welfare. A comprehensive indicator of the economic status of families or individuals would strengthen definitions of horizontal and vertical equity. These improvements should, for example, aid in identifying who among the population are poor. Moreover, the development of a broad measure of economic welfare provides a valuable framework for a study of the redistributional impact of various government taxes and expenditures. Unless families can be adequately ranked by level of economic status, the effectiveness of programs with redistributional goals cannot be determined.

An accurate indicator of economic status should capture a family's command over all goods and services. By this criterion, the traditional money income measure is obviously inadequate. Families at the same income level may vary substantially in their ability to consume goods and services. Both the absolute amount of resources and the ranking of families by economic status are likely to change if a more comprehensive measure is adopted. Thus the poor, as classified by an expanded measure, should differ substantially from the money income poor in both size and particular families included.

This monograph develops a comprehensive measure of economic welfare which captures the yearly potential consumption for families,

1

consistent with a life-cycle hypothesis of savings.[1] The subsequent distributional ranking of families by this measure is used to evaluate the effectiveness of eleven different tax expenditure and transfer programs. Although distributional studies do not usually single out one subgroup of the population, this research derives a measure of economic status particularly directed at aged families.

While much of the analysis undertaken here is appropriate to the population as a whole, the development of a comprehensive indicator of economic welfare should be sensitive to families' economic circumstances. The needs and resources of the elderly pose unique problems. It is especially appropriate for the aged to be the first group for such a study. Money income is a less important source of economic well-being for elderly families, many of whom receive no earned income. Moreover, aged families and individuals receive a higher proportion of government tax expenditure and transfer programs than any other group in the United States. In 1971, over $47.2 billion of the total $79.7 billion expended on federal income security programs went to persons aged sixty-five and older (U.S., Bureau of the Budget 1972, p. 188).[2] Yet even with such massive transfer programs the aged continue to have a higher incidence of money income poverty than any other age group; in 1972, 18.6 percent of all persons sixty-five and over were below the poverty threshold lines established by the Social Security Administration (U.S., Bureau of the Census 1973, p. 63). Given the magnitude and recent rapid growth of these government income security programs, economists and policy makers need the best possible tools to assess their impact on the economic welfare of aged families.

To demonstrate further the importance of dealing separately with elderly families and to define more precisely the group under study, the following section briefly profiles the aged. The socioeconomic characteristics presented illustrate the needs and resources of the elderly segment of the population and set the stage for much of the analysis to follow. Since the measure developed here is confined to the aged, it is also important to note disparities in these characteristics between this group and the population as a whole. The emphasis in the measure of economic status would change when applied to a broader segment of the population.

---

[1] As used in this study, the term *family* includes unrelated individuals as well as two or more related individuals.

[2] Income security programs include all cash and in-kind transfers of the federal government and "tax expenditures" found in the federal personal income tax. Tax expenditures refer to provisions in the tax laws which reduce the liabilities for various groups within the population.

A PROFILE OF THE AGED

The first step in this analysis is to identify the exact group of the population under study. When does an individual qualify as aged? The most commonly used definition is someone sixty-five years of age or older. This alternative represents the age of eligibility for full Social Security benefits, Medicare, Supplemental Security Income, and other government and private retirement-related programs. In 1972, this definition included 20.7 million persons in the United States, almost 10 percent of the total population (U.S., Bureau of the Census 1973, pp. 64, 66). A less frequently employed limit is age sixty-two or over, the age at which persons first become eligible for reduced Social Security benefits. Under this definition, the number of aged persons would increase by nearly 20 percent. Since for many the term "aged" is synonymous with "retired," a third possibility is to define an aged person as one who has left the labor force, perhaps with some lower bound on age. Indeed, two retired persons of different ages may have more in common than two persons of the same age, one of whom remains in the labor force. This approach would reduce the number of individuals included for any given age. Although none of these three definitions can necessarily be considered "correct," this study employs the "age sixty-five and over" alternative.

The basic unit for this study is the family. The composition of the aged family unit defined here includes individuals residing alone as well as those in larger units, and families in which one or more members are sixty-five or over.[3] The usual definition of aged family, in which the head has to be at least sixty-five, understates the total, since a substantial number of aged persons reside with relatives. Thus, these elderly individuals usually escape our attention. This study attempts to measure the economic welfare of all the aged and thus includes persons sixty-five and over regardless of their living arrangements. In 1972, families with an aged head of household comprised 19.8 percent of all families. The expanded definition raises this proportion to 22 percent. Thus, families headed by younger adults but with aged relatives present totaled nearly 10 percent of all families with any member over sixty-five in 1972. Moreover, families headed by aged individuals with additional young adult members accounted for another 12.4 percent of elderly families as defined here.[4]

[3] When the Census combines families and unrelated individuals, it defines the resulting category as a "household."

[4] This information was calculated from tape files of the U.S. Bureau of the Census Current Population Survey for 1972. Unless otherwise specified, all remaining family statistics for 1972 are derived from this source.

TABLE 1.1
Demographic Characteristics of Families, 1972

Demographic Characteristic	Head or Spouse 65 or Over	Families with Young Head and Spouse	
		With Aged Member(s)	No Aged Members
Proportion of families	19.78%	2.19%	78.03%
Average family size	1.75	4.02	3.16
Sex of head			
Male	58.08%	75.73%	81.17%
Female	41.92	24.27	18.83
Marital status			
Single (never married)	6.51	17.38	11.17%
Married	45.58	60.88	70.12
Other	47.91	21.73	18.72
Race of head			
White	90.77	88.40	87.89%
Black	8.37	10.60	10.71
Other	.86	1.00	1.41
Average education of head	9.25 yrs.	11.32 yrs.	11.80 yrs.
Region of residence			
Northeast	25.01%	31.55%	23.25%
North Central	27.22	24.69	27.05
South	31.48	30.05	30.71
West	16.29	13.71	18.46
Location of residence			
Central city	33.45	34.85	32.81%
Urban fringe	29.79	40.27	37.59
Not SMSA*	36.76	24.88	29.60

SOURCE: Calculated from U.S. Bureau of the Census Current Population Survey computer tapes for 1972.
* SMSA = Standard Metropolitan Statistical Areas as defined by U.S. Office of Management and Budget.

Table 1.1 displays the demographic characteristics of aged and young families. Those families not normally classified as aged but included in the definition for this study are shown separately. Aged families (column 1) are smaller, more often headed by a woman, and tend to reside outside metropolitan areas. The head of an aged household is less likely to be married, nonwhite, or a high school graduate. Certainly these findings are not surprising. Because of the aging process and differences in life expectancies, many widowed, aged persons (especially women) reside alone. Moreover, lower education levels and place of residence often reflect decisions made many years earlier. It is also important to note the differences between families with aged members headed by young adults and those without. The former tend to be larger, undoubtedly reflecting their "extended" family structure. Moreover, more of these family heads are women and unmarried than is the case for families with no aged members. This may be an indication of the convenience to younger members of having an elderly relative in the household.

In addition to this general demographic information, some other characteristics illustrate crucial concerns in the development of an economic status measure for aged families. For the elderly, health status is likely to be an important determinant of need. Illness can cause withdrawal from the labor force and a change in living arrangements, as well as induce large medical bills. The 1963 Social Security Survey of the Aged found that poor health was the principal reason given for retirement by 53 percent of all men who left the labor force between the ages of sixty-two and sixty-four and by 41 percent of all men who retired at age sixty-five or over (Epstein and Murray 1967, pp. 345–46). The potential financial burden of poor health can also be illustrated by the mean amount spent each year on medical care by elderly persons. For fiscal 1973 the average aged person spent $1,052 on health care, with 64 percent of this amount paid by public programs. The individual bore the remaining $379 privately. Moreover, a comparison of health care expenditures between those over sixty-five and the younger population indicated that the aged spent nearly three times more per capita on health than younger persons (Cooper and Piro 1974). The needs of the aged in this area are substantial.

Although medical expenses for the aged are large, improved medical care has helped extend the life expectancy of elderly persons. This expansion is reflected in the changes in age distribution among those sixty-five and over. Thirty-four percent of all aged persons were seventy-five or over in 1960. By 1970, this group accounted for fully 38 percent of all elderly individuals (Chen 1971, pp. 11–12). Yet at the same time, the age of retirement is decreasing. In 1965, 14.3 million persons, 82 percent of the total population sixty-five and over, were out of the labor force. This figure grew to 17.3 million in 1973, or 85 percent of all elderly persons (U.S., Bureau of Labor Statistics 1974, pp. 32, 36). An even more revealing figure is the significant reduction in the proportion of men aged sixty-five through sixty-nine in the labor force. In 1950, 59.8 percent were still labor force participants. The rate fell to 42.6 percent in 1964 (Kreps 1971, p. 70). The expansion of early retirement provisions for Social Security to include men between the ages of sixty-two and sixty-four has reduced the age of retirement.

TABLE 1.2
Components of Income by Age of Head, 1972

Age of Family Head	Mean Income	Standard-ized Mean Income*	Sources of Income (As Percentage of Total)					
			Earnings	Property Income	Social Security	Welfare, Public Assis-tance	Remain-ing Trans-fers	Other Income
41–55	$14,155.19	$16,292.77	92.26%	2.99%	1.39%	.55%	2.18%	.91%
56–61	12,087.97	16,825.68	87.57	5.44	2.41	.62	2.86	1.44
62–64	9841.29	14,817.03	76.64	7.65	7.65	.77	4.00	3.35
65–69	7432.93	12,272.01	49.95	12.78	24.01	1.11	4.91	7.54
70–74	5895.25	10,182.78	31.56	18.35	35.76	1.63	5.88	7.46
75–79	5237.44	9075.45	26.30	17.65	40.03	1.83	7.17	7.14
80–99	4566.42	8158.97	22.85	22.70	39.06	2.88	6.50	6.03

SOURCE: Calculated from Current Population Survey computer tapes for 1972.
* Income is standardized as if all families had four members. See footnote 5.

Pechman, Aaron, and Taussig (1968, pp. 132–33) noted a significant drop in labor force participation for this group between 1961 and 1966. Thus, as a result of longer life expectancies and reduced labor market participation, the number of persons dependent upon sources of income other than earnings is obviously increasing over time. Hence, the role of transfers and their distributional impact should assume even greater importance.

Variations in current income between those over sixty-five and the younger population illustrate why it is important to develop an expanded measure of economic status for elderly families. For the aged, average income is lower, more are below the poverty threshold levels, and sources of income are different from those for the rest of the population. Table 1.2 illustrates several trends in the size and sources of income among families with different-aged household heads. Incomes fall dramatically as the age of family heads increases. From its highest point for the forty-one to fifty-five-year-old age group, mean income declines until, for the eighty to ninety-nine-year-old heads, it comprises only 32 percent of the income of the younger group. However, if incomes are controlled for family size, the incomes of the oldest group are slightly more than half the size of those of the forty-one to fifty-five-year-old age group.[5] The importance of earnings declines steadily for older family heads, showing the steepest drop around the traditional retirement age of sixty-five.

Although all other income sources rise in importance, they do not nearly replace lost earnings. Some of the increases in the share of these nonearned sources are due merely to the fact that the absolute amount of earnings falls so dramatically. The inadequacy of income replacement by other sources when an earner retires accounts for much of the decline in mean income. Moreover, it is important to note that property income rises both proportionally and in absolute dollars for aged families, underscoring the potential size of the asset holdings of the aged.

An alternative view of these income characteristics is summarized in table 1.3. Again families are divided into three categories: where the head or spouse is aged, where some other family member is sixty-five or older, and where there are no aged members. Standardized mean income shows less variation among the three categories than does simple mean income. This standardization reflects the differ-

[5] To compare families of varying size, the level of income for each family is multiplied by a weighting factor. In this case, the procedure standardizes income to a level comparable to the income of a family of four. The weight is obtained by dividing the 1972 poverty threshold for a family of four by each family's appropriate poverty threshold.

TABLE 1.3
Income Characteristics of Families, 1972

Income Characteristics	Head or Spouse 65 or Over	Families with Young Head and Spouse	
		With Aged Member(s)	No Aged Members
Mean income	$ 6172.03	$14,807.24	$11,765.20
Standardized mean income*	10,460.74	15,655.96	14,427.38
Components of income			
Earnings	38.69%	80.88%	92.36%
Property income	16.14	4.17	2.78
Social Security	31.13	8.83	1.17
Welfare, Public assistance	1.57	1.18	.88
Remaining transfers	5.73	2.52	1.96
Other income	7.13	1.63	1.10
Families under poverty threshold			
Before transfers	62.04%	14.91%	15.62%
After transfers	22.74	6.17	11.99
Mean income of aged members	$ 5738.57	$ 2445.89	—

SOURCE: Calculated from U.S. Bureau of the Census Current Population Survey computer tapes for 1972.
* Income is standardized as if all families had four members. See footnote 5.

ences in family size. Aged families are smaller, so that when standardized, mean incomes for this group rise. Earnings are less than half as important to aged families as a source of income than to either of the young family categories. Social Security and the "remaining" transfers—which include government and veterans' pensions—are substantially more important. This is further illustrated by the percentage of pre- and posttransfer poor in each category. The last income characteristic in the table, mean income of aged members, is an adjusted figure for income when there is at least one young adult present in the household who is not the spouse of an aged member. This figure includes only the income of the aged portion of the family and thus only differs from mean income for those families with young adult members. In the second column, all families' incomes must be separated to establish the amount attributable to the aged "subfamily."[6] The contrasts in demographic characteristics between young families with and without aged members are striking. The presence of aged relatives increases the importance of transfer income to the young.

[6] Because of limitations on the data available, income of aged members for column 2 may be understated when family size is very large.

THE APPROACH

Chapter 2 develops a theoretical framework for a more comprehensive measure of economic welfare. The definition developed for this research includes resources available for consumption in a particular time period, consistent with a life-cycle hypothesis for saving. This measure will capture the family's effective resource constraint, which in turn is modified to reflect the family's own evaluation of each component and then adjusted for family needs. Among the important potential sources of economic welfare other than current income for aged families are: an annual share of net worth, the net contribution of government, intrafamily transfers, and the value of leisure and non-market-productive activities.

In chapter 3 an empirical measure of economic welfare based on the formal discussion in chapter 2 is developed. Theoretical considerations, as well as the feasibility of developing empirical estimates, dictate the components of this measure. The estimation procedures for each component are discussed in detail. Chapter 4 presents the results of these calculations and examines the contribution of each component to the ranking of families and to summary measures of inequality. To emphasize the power of the new measure, comparisons are made between the complete measure of economic welfare and current money income. Demographic characteristics of those at the bottom of each distribution conclude chapter 4.

Chapter 5 uses the new economic status measure to estimate the distributional impact of a broad range of important transfer and tax expenditure programs. The specific cash transfers included are Social Security and Railroad Retirement, government employee and retirement programs, veterans' disability pensions and compensation, unemployment insurance and workmen's compensation, and public assistance. In-kind transfers include Medicare, Medicaid, and public housing. Finally, specific tax expenditure programs targeted at the aged—the double personal exemption, exclusion of Social Security and other transfer income, and the retirement income tax credit—are also incorporated. Altogether, these programs represented the most important transfers to the aged in 1967. Comparisons by measure and by program provide a number of insights into the contribution of these transfers to the well-being of aged families.

2

The Theoretical Measure of Economic Welfare

Economists often view the link between economic theory and the definition of economic welfare as extremely tenuous. The invalidity of interpersonal utility comparisons has caused many researchers to ignore consumer theory and instead simply use current money income as a proxy for a measure of economic welfare. This chapter presents a more comprehensive measure of economic status, incorporating the important resources available to an aged family into a utility theory framework.[1] While the theoretical measure cannot in practice be totally quantified, it does provide a guide for significant improvements over the current money income definition. Since the indicator of economic status developed here is applied specifically to aged families, this research places its emphasis on sources of well-being most crucial for this subgroup of the population. Although the analysis in general

[1] A caveat about economic welfare should be given. The ideal measure of economic welfare for a family is the level of satisfaction reached as measured by its utility function. However, even if such a measure were attainable, the limitations of standard consumer theory prevent comparisons of the magnitude of one family's preferences against any other family's preferences. Neither ordinal nor cardinal rankings can be obtained. In this sense, then, economic welfare may never be truly measurable. This should not, however, be viewed as a counsel of despair. Comparisons among families by current money income are often used in distributional studies as crude approximations of economic welfare. The measure developed here can certainly improve upon a money income ranking of families.

11

should be valid for the entire population, the specific components of economic welfare should vary somewhat for other subgroups. For example, for population groups where earned income is a principal source of well-being or where human capital is more important than physical assets held, more attention should be devoted to the specification of the earnings component.

Moreover, the measure of economic welfare for the aged proposed here is *not* intended for comparison with the current income positions of the rest of the population. Until similar definitions of economic welfare have been estimated for other groups which take into account their specific needs and resources, the use of this measure should be confined to comparisons among the aged. However, even within such a restricted framework, the measure can be beneficial in answering questions about the effectiveness of various transfer and tax expenditure programs. This research also provides the first step toward the creation of a more sensitive measure of economic welfare for the entire population.

ECONOMIC WELFARE

A fully comprehensive measure of economic welfare poses many difficult conceptual issues which are most appropriately viewed within a standard utility function framework. Resources which extend the budget constraint of a family increase its potential consumption, subject to preferences expressed through the family's utility function. The measure of economic welfare developed here concentrates on the family's resource constraint. Such a measure reflects the level of attainable (rather than attained) consumption by a family. According to Harold Watts, such an indicator of economic status is "a property of the individual's situation, rather than a characteristic of the individual or of his pattern of behavior" (1969, p. 371).

Although this study examines economic welfare at only one point in time, the statement of utility maximization nonetheless is consistent with the Ando–Modigliani–Brumberg life-cycle hypothesis of saving (Ando and Modigliani 1963). Utility is treated as a function of consumption in both current and future time periods and is maximized subject to the resources available to an individual over time. These resources include total net worth, current earnings and other nonproperty income, and the discounted value of all future nonproperty income expected over the person's remaining lifetime. The present value of total resources (PV_0) is defined by the following formula:

$$PV_0 = A_0 + Y_0^n + \sum_{t=1}^{N} \frac{EY_t^n}{(1+r)^t}$$

where

A_0 = stocks of assets at the beginning of present period
Y_0^n = current nonproperty income in period $t = 0$
EY_t^n = expected nonproperty income in period t
N = years of life expectancy for individual
r = rate of return on assets.

Consumption in any given time period is proportional to the present value of the total resource flow accruing to an individual over the remaining years of life. The exact proportion devoted to consumption in each time period depends on the age of the person, the rate of return on assets, and the form of the utility function. Consumption in any period t is expressed as

$$C_t = \gamma_t PV_t$$

where

C_t = consumption in period t
γ_t = the proportionality factor for period t.

The assumption that γ_t allocates an equal proportional share of lifetime resources in each period t lends simplicity to the analysis. Moreover, if in any time period, current nonproperty income (Y_t^n) is exogenous, then only assets and expected future nonproperty income can be altered to yield the appropriate level for C_t. For any one year, the amount of assets consumed through saving or dissaving would reflect expectations about future nonproperty income. Consequently, the level of potential consumption (C_t), consistent with the life-cycle model, is disaggregated as

$$C_t = Y_t^n + S_t$$

where
S_t = the portion of net worth available for consumption during the period.

Y_t^n, current nonproperty income as defined above, is assumed to be exogenous for any period t. Thus, S_t is the share of net worth which ensures that current consumption is consistent with the lifetime utility function. The determinants of S_t are as follows:

$$S_t = f(A_t, \gamma_t, EY_t^n, r, N).$$

EY_t^n influences S_t through its size and stability over time in comparison to the size of Y_t^n. For example, if future expected nonproperty income equals current nonproperty income in all subsequent periods (and since consumption has already been assumed to be equal across all periods), then S_t would also be the same for all t and depend only on the size of assets and the values for life expectancy (N) and the interest rate (r). Thus, S_t becomes a constant annuity, expressed as

$$S_t = A_t \left(\frac{r}{1 - (1 + r)^{-N}} \right).$$

However, if EY_t^n were expected to decrease over time, then to maintain consumption at a constant level, S_t should increase. In this case, S_t would correspond to a variable annuity formulation such that the current share of assets would be small relative to later periods.[2]

Although the life-cycle hypothesis was originally formulated only for current nonproperty income and net worth, this study expands the scope of the resources included. Resources which either provide goods directly, or through some other means allow an individual command over goods and services, can appropriately be viewed as increasing potential consumption. This study treats these components of economic welfare in the same manner as nonproperty income, incorporating both current and expected future benefits into the resource constraint. For example, government provided commodities, leisure time, and nonmarket produced goods all enhance the level of utility enjoyed by a family. Thus, the measure of economic welfare (W_t) is best defined as

$$W_t = \hat{C}_t = \hat{Y}_t + S_t$$

where

$\hat{C}_t$ = "expanded" current potential consumption
$\hat{Y}_t$ = all current net inflows of resources available for consumption (except property income).

This measure of economic status expands the resource constraint faced by families beyond measured current money income. A complete listing of resources which provide utility could incorporate "intangible" commodities for aged families. This component might include such things as proximity of adult children, levels of noise or air pollution, or some even less specific notions of "happiness." Problems in quantify-

---

[2] Although the issue is not addressed here, S_t could also be negative, indicating income greater than consumption. Such a formulation might be appropriate for younger families, but S_t is implicitly assumed to be positive or zero for aged families.

ing and measuring these aspects of economic welfare preclude their inclusion.

The Specific Components

Since money income forms the basis for the life-cycle hypothesis and most distributional work, the development of the components of economic welfare can appropriately begin with current income. Those portions of income which provide only limited information about total available resources are expanded into broader components. Current income, divided into its several parts, can be viewed as

$$Y_t = Y_t^e + Y_t^u + G_t^c + O_t$$

where

Y_t = total current income in period t

Y_t^e = earned income in period t

Y_t^u = property income including dividends, interest, and rental payments

G_t^c = government cash transfers

O_t = other components of current income including cash gifts from relatives, private pension payments, and royalties.

Current income includes portions of additional, important resource flows. For example, property income is, in part, a function of the amount of net worth owned by the family. But ownership of assets by an aged family adds more to potential consumption, and hence economic welfare, than is indicated by property income. An annual share of net worth (S_t), apportioned so as not to "prematurely" draw down total net assets, best replaces property income (Y_t^u).

Another important component of economic welfare only partially captured by current income is the contribution of government (G_t). Most current income measures include the value of cash transfer payments (G_t^c). However, all aspects of government taxes and expenditures may influence the level of welfare of aged families. The total incidence of government is thus a major component of the resource constraint.

The third aspect of economic welfare understated in measured current income is aid from relatives. Current money income measures include cash gifts from relatives outside the nuclear family. An even more important source, however, is *intra*family aid, often in the form of an in-kind transfer. These intrafamily transfers occur when an aged individual or family resides with younger relatives and when one of the family units (either young or old) that comprises the extended family has a proportionately higher level of resources relative to its needs than the other.

The value of non-market-productive activities and leisure time provides yet another source of potential consumption by the aged. The output of home produced goods and other nonpaid but productive activities enhance the level of well-being of a family. Moreover, if leisure is considered a normal good, then the consumption of leisure time should also enter the family's utility function, regardless of whether any good or service is produced. Leisure time (L_t)—including the value of nonmarket production—can be viewed as a single component of economic welfare.

Once all the resources available for consumption during the time period have been assembled, some standardization for needs among families is necessary to facilitate a ranking. Adjustments for family size, composition, and location of residence are among the more obvious types of standardization. However, accounting for special needs, such as for health, may be even more important to individual families. The measure of welfare should thus be adjusted for family needs (λ).

Thus, the complete theoretical measure of economic welfare can be expressed as

$$W_t = (\hat{Y}_t + S_t)\lambda$$
$$\hat{Y}_t = Y_t^e + O_t + G_t + I_t + L_t.$$

With this specification of the current resource component $(\hat{Y}_t)$, only earnings (Y_t^e) and "other" income (O_t) remain unchanged from current money income. The measures of government (G_t) and the share of net worth (S_t) have absorbed cash transfers (G_t^c) and property income (Y_t^u), respectively. Measures of intrafamily transfers (I_t) and leisure and non-market-productive activities (L_t) complete the resources available to a family for potential consumption. In addition, an adjustment (λ) standardizes the equation for each family's needs. The size of S_t in each period depends upon the components of $\hat{Y}_t$. Even if each separate component changes, as long as the total effect is a stable $\hat{Y}_t$, S_t will also be constant. The remainder of this chapter discusses each component separately, examining its expected size and stability, problems of estimation, and anticipated distributional effects.

EARNED INCOME

The inclusion of earned income in a measure of economic welfare requires no lengthy justification. For the population as a whole, wages, salaries, and business and farm income contribute the bulk of current money income and thus are perhaps the most important single indicator of the well-being of a family. For those over sixty-five, however, earned income constitutes only about 30 percent of current money income (Bixby 1970). Nonetheless, the existence of this income is important to an aged family's level of economic welfare. On average, persons still in the labor force after age sixty-five have a higher total current money income than individuals of the same age not in the labor force (Epstein and Murray 1967). Several reasons can be offered. First, there are almost no "income replacement" plans in the private or public sectors which fully compensate for the loss of income upon retirement. In addition, many of those outside the labor force have not voluntarily retired; they currently suffer—and perhaps to an even greater degree—the same problems that have plagued them throughout life: ill health, low skills, and discrimination, for example. It is thus natural to expect retired persons also to have lower alternative income sources, such as property income, reflecting the level of previous earnings.

The stability of this source of economic welfare is also of concern. For younger families within the aged category (i.e., those between sixty-five and seventy) with at least one member in the labor force, projecting the same level of income to future periods is likely to overstate income. For older persons, labor force participation rates steadily decline. Consequently, these families can expect lower earned incomes in some future period. Just as all assets should not be included as a component of current economic welfare, total expected earnings should also be allocated over the remaining lifetime of a family. That is, the life-cycle model requires that not all current earned income be attributed to current economic welfare if earnings are expected to fall over time (and a constant level of consumption is desired in each year). However, it is possible that when all the resources constituting $\hat{Y}_t$ are taken into account, the change in S_t might be mitigated. To the extent that other resources increase when an aged person leaves the labor force—e.g., pensions and the dollar value of leisure time—they may partially compensate for the reduction in earnings.

OTHER INCOME

"Other income" is a residual category for current money income from private sources after deducting earnings and payments from dividends, interest, and rent. It captures increases in the level of economic welfare from such sources as interfamily cash gifts, private pensions, annuities, and royalties. The most important of these sources is private pension payments. Although this portion of income is still limited, private pensions have grown rapidly in recent years and will continue to gain importance as a component of economic welfare. In 1950, when private programs were just beginning, there were only 450,000 beneficiaries. By 1968, the number had risen to 3.8 million persons receiving over $5 billion in benefits (Chen 1971, p. 36). During this eighteen-year period, the proportion of private pension recipients grew from 3.7 to 19.6 percent of all aged individuals. Those who currently receive benefits can expect a constant stream over their remaining lifetimes. Moreover, individuals who are eligible for benefits but who have not yet retired will be able to use these pensions as a partial substitute for lost earnings. Thus, private pension benefits tend to stabilize the flow of current resources when added to the welfare equation.[3]

Cash grants from relatives outside the household comprise another component of "other" income. Their limited size—between 1 and 3 percent of current money income—can be explained in several ways (Bixby 1970, p. 11). Government programs have undoubtedly eased the responsibility of families to care for their elderly members. Moreover, a substantial minority of the aged live with younger relatives, so that for this group, aid is confined within the home in the form of shared income or household services. Since grants from relatives outside the home are so small and expectations about future gifts may well remain constant, current gifts received (and given) can simply be added to (or subtracted from) the measure.

GOVERNMENT TAXES AND EXPENDITURES

Government taxes and expenditures play a substantial role in determining the distribution of economic welfare. In fiscal 1973, government expenditures at all levels totaled more than $250 billion—almost one-fourth of national income for 1973 (Schultze et al. 1972, p. 7). Moreover, because benefits and tax liabilities vary among the population, such large expenditures are certain to affect the distribution of economic welfare. Aged persons receive a disproportionately large share of total cash and in-kind transfers. In 1971, over half of all transfers and tax expenditures were granted to aged families (U.S., Bureau

---

[3] Current private pension contributions should be subtracted from resources available for consumption to maintain consistency.

of the Budget 1972, p. 186). Moreover, cash transfers alone constitute almost 44 percent of the current money income of persons over age sixty-five (Bixby 1970, p. 11).

The stability of the contribution of government over time is difficult to determine. Although the size of federal, state, and local government expenditures has increased dramatically in the past, the *net* impact of government per person over the entire population may remain fairly constant. However, subgroups within the population are probably affected more by the proportion of the budget devoted to various programs and the share of the revenue borne by various types of taxes. If the distributional effects of these taxes and expenditures vary by level of economic welfare and demographic categories, then changes in the composition of the budget may alter the relative yearly contribution of government to a family's level of economic welfare.

For example, in recent years both cash and in-kind transfers have increased absolutely and as a percentage of the total budget (Schultze et al. 1972, pp. 10–14). Since aged families receive a large portion of such benefits, it might be expected that G_t to this group has been increasing over time. However, on a year-to-year basis, drastic changes seldom occur. What changes do take place appear quite small when divided among the aged population, which has also been growing over time. As indicated above, the impact of government can be broken down into four subcomponents: (1) cash transfers, (2) in-kind transfers, (3) direct government expenditures on goods and services, and (4) taxes. These four aspects are discussed separately below.

Cash Transfers

Cash transfers have an immediate and dramatic effect on the distribution of economic welfare among the aged. The importance of this source of well-being cannot be overemphasized. Two separate objectives are often cited in granting public monetary transfers to the aged: first, Social Security and government employees' retirement benefits are aimed at the aged of all income levels in order to partially replace earnings lost upon retirement; second, a large portion of those aged falling below a certain money income level are given aid through Supplemental Security Income and, formerly, through Old Age Assistance or general assistance programs to raise their living standards above some minimum level.

Once a family has become eligible for any of these programs, it is likely to remain so. Increases in benefits to current recipients occur mainly to adjust for cost-of-living changes. Thus, for current recipient families this source of income should be reasonably constant over time. On the other hand, some families who currently receive few benefits can expect higher levels in the future as family members retire. To the extent that these programs effectively compensate for lost earnings, they may be viewed as stabilizing expectations about future consumption.[4]

In-Kind Transfers

As is the case with cash transfers, in-kind programs are directed toward at least two target groups among the aged. Almost anyone over sixty-five may qualify for Medicare, while other programs are directed at those below a certain income level (e.g., public housing, Medicaid). Moreover, these programs concentrate on basic needs, notably medical care, housing, and food. Expenditures on the Medicare and Medicaid programs for the aged totaled more than $9.4 billion in 1971, while remaining in-kind transfers provided $396 million in benefits to the aged (U.S., Bureau of the Budget 1972, p. 188). Although these other programs are limited in scope, specific recipients of food programs and public housing may receive substantial benefits. Moreover, by 1974, the size of the Food Stamp program had mushroomed (Skolnik and Dales 1975).

Unlike measuring cash transfer payments (which can be added directly to other cash flows), measuring benefits from in-kind programs involves difficult conceptual issues. The simplest approach—and that advocated by Irwin Gillespie (1965)—values benefits as "costs incurred on behalf of" recipients. The assumption that benefits equal costs eliminates most of the measurement problems and has the virtue of simplicity. A second treatment would be to set benefits at their private market values. For in-kind transfers, a comparable privately provided good or service can usually be identified. Market values represent the cost of the good or service to a consumer if he had to purchase it through the private market. For a number of reasons, this might not coincide with the cost of publicly providing the goods.[5]

However, both of the above alternatives ignore some important issues in valuing in-kind transfers. As Schmundt, Smolensky, and Stiefel (1975) have noted, the value that the recipients themselves place on transfer benefits may well be substantially less than either the

---

[4] Again, the slack may be taken up by adjustment of savings or dissavings of net worth.

[5] The consequences of this and other alternatives on the valuation of public housing are discussed in Smolensky and Gomery (1973, pp. 147–52).

market price or cost through the public sector. When an in-kind transfer provides a good at a lower or zero price, and if it enters positively into the recipient's utility function, the recipient is made better off. However, the price change resulting from subsidization of a good usually places the individual on an indifference curve that can be reached with a smaller cash grant. Measured in dollar terms, then, the value of the transfer to the recipient is positive, but not as high as the cost of providing it.[6] There are several exceptions to this, such as when the indifference curves are either linear (perfect substitution with other goods) or rectangular (goods consumed in fixed proportions). Also, if the subsidized good is granted only in fixed quantities and the quantity is the amount the recipient would consume were he to receive a cash transfer, the good will be valued at its full market price. For the more common case, Schmundt, Smolensky, and Stiefel (1975) developed a procedure for valuing in-kind transfers in "equivalent (real income equivalent) cash transfer units." This approach requires specification of a utility function and knowledge about each family's level of disposable cash income and the combination of in-kind programs available.

In addition, a large program can cause price increases which, in turn, affect incomes of both recipients and nonrecipients of a particular transfer policy. For example, the Medicare and Medicaid programs may have caused increased medical prices, creating a greater burden on those not receiving program benefits and on those recipients who must bear the cost of the uninsured portion of their expenses. The solution would be to employ a general equilibrium framework to incorporate changes in relative factor and commodity prices in the resource constraint. A higher price would result in lower potential consumption and, hence, lower W_t for each family.

Direct Government Expenditures

Direct expenditures on goods and services by the public sector can have an important influence on the level of economic welfare of any group. Certainly few government programs can claim to be distributionally neutral. The estimation of the distributional consequences of government expenditures entails many of the same problems faced in the estimation of in-kind transfer benefits. For example, an ideal measure of government's impact on economic welfare should value benefits as they enter a family's utility function. In addition, most

---

[6] This analysis is analogous to the excise–income tax debates found, for example, in Joseph (1939) and Little (1951).

government expenditures are not directed at particular recipients. Gillespie (1965) is one of the few researchers to have attempted a comprehensive examination of the effect of government expenditures on the distribution of income.[7] He concentrated on those "expenditures the costs of which are incurred on behalf of clearly delineated beneficiary groups, whether they are consumers or suppliers of factors" (p. 130). Gillespie estimated distributions for the population as a whole. The same distributional relationships may not exist among the aged. Moreover, since Gillespie's study uses current money income as the measure of economic welfare, the expanded definition proposed here should also result in different distributional effects.

Taxes

As the means for financing most government programs, tax liabilities need to be estimated to obtain the net effects of government on the distribution of economic welfare. Moreover, governments can manipulate taxes to achieve various distributional goals by controlling both the tax base and the rate structure. For example, special exemptions and deductions—the "tax expenditures"—contained in the federal personal income tax yield implicit subsidies to various groups of taxpayers to meet such distributional goals.[8] Public finance contains an extensive literature on the incidence of taxation. The final burden or incidence of a tax may be quite different from its initial impact, depending upon assumptions about tax shifting. The corporate income tax, excise, and payroll taxes are among those most frequently examined.[9]

Heretofore, researchers have measured the distributional effects of taxes by income class. For example, Gillespie (1965), Bishop (1967), and Reynolds and Smolensky (1974) have synthesized studies done by others in order to calculate total tax incidence for families by current money income. For taxes based on income, such a method is reasonable. However, also included in these studies are property and estate taxes, which depend upon a person's asset holdings. These taxes may vary substantially among families within any single current money income bracket.

A more recent and comprehensive study of tax incidence by Pechman and Okner (1974) attempted to correct some of these prob-

---

[7] See also Bishop (1967) and Reynolds and Smolensky (1974).

[8] These tax expenditure programs are discussed in more detail in chapter 5, where the distributional effects of three such provisions are estimated.

[9] A discussion of shifting and incidence and references to important studies of these taxes can be found in Pechman (1971).

lems. They used a merged data base combining information from the Survey of Economic Opportunity and the Internal Revenue Service file on individual income tax returns. With this data set, they were able to undertake more sophisticated incidence calculations using several different sets of assumptions. Pechman and Okner found little difference in the incidence of taxes between their most progressive and least progressive calculations. In fact, they concluded that little redistribution results when all taxes are taken into account. Aged families pay slightly lower taxes overall, but again, within this group taxes are not particularly redistributive.

INTRAFAMILY TRANSFERS

The living arrangements of aged persons can have a direct bearing on the level and stability of their economic welfare. Nonmonetary transfers of resources within extended family units constitute the principal source of aid to the aged by relatives. A substantial minority of those over sixty-five are in a position to receive intrafamily transfers through their living arrangements. The 1968 Social Security Survey of the Aged estimated that 19 percent of all aged couples and 38 percent of nonmarried aged persons (widowed, divorced, separated, or never married) lived with relatives (Murray 1971, p. 5). In the majority of cases, these relatives included their adult children.

Economic incentives are among the most important motives for such extended families. This is usually a simpler, more efficient way of providing for needy relatives than supporting them in separate households. Moreover, there may be economies of scale associated with the resulting larger family. Morgan et al. (1962, pp. 158–78) found that most people they interviewed disapprove of such living arrangements and bring relatives into the household only when it becomes necessary to provide support. Their study concluded that 73 percent of the dependent "extra adult units" improved their economic situation by living with relatives, and that only 5 percent of those units were worse off than if they lived alone.

Previous attempts at estimating the size of intrafamily transfers have been quite limited. In general, research has only concentrated on identifying aged persons most likely to be receiving such transfers. The 1963 Social Security Survey of the Aged found that elderly couples and nonmarried aged women were the most likely to reside with relatives.[10] Except for a tendency for persons with the lowest

---

[10] See, for example, Murray (1971).

incomes to live in extended families, such arrangements did not vary consistently with income. Those living alone did seem to have higher liquid assets than those living with relatives, but the same result did not follow for homeownership. However, the survey did not examine the level of income and assets of the other (nonaged) relatives in the extended family. Without such information, it would not be possible to predict why the aged resided in these larger units. The disparity in income and assets among families probably reveals more about living arrangements than does the absolute level of income of aged families. The 1968 Survey of the Aged did gather data on relatives' incomes (Epstein and Murray 1967). However, there was so large an underreporting problem that, to date, no further analysis has been attempted.

Steiner and Dorfman (1957) attempted to glean some information on the contributions of living arrangements to the economic status of the aged even though they too lacked information on the resources of relatives with whom aged persons reside. The authors attempted to give some indication of the direction of nonmonetary aid by examining the resources of older persons when subdivided into three groups: aged persons who live apart from relatives, aged persons residing with relatives where an aged member is designated the head, and finally, aged persons in an extended family where one of the younger members is listed as head. In the last case the income of aged members was quite low, indicating a probable dependence on others. With no information on the resources of younger relatives, Steiner and Dorfman could only suggest the possible influence of such living arrangements. Morgan et al. (1962, p. 492) actually calculated a measure of intrafamily transfers. They estimated the value of food and housing that the dependent subfamily might receive from living with relatives. These estimates were then added to reported cash gifts for the net intrafamily transfer. Thus, this measure provides a conservative estimate of the subsistence needs supplied by the primary family unit, although it is not directly linked with size of each family's income.

Perhaps the most important study for this research is that of Baerwaldt and Morgan (1973). Although they did not specifically deal with aged or extended families, the authors did estimate flows of income and resources among all family members, and this sometimes included aged relatives. The study is of great interest because it attempted to estimate an actual dollar amount for transfers among family members and provided some guidelines for the allocation of these transfers. For several different variants of income, Baerwaldt and Morgan allocated income to family members via three methods: (1) on a per capita basis, (2) in proportion to physical needs as measured by food requirements, and (3) in proportion to needs with additional assumptions about savings behavior for persons above a certain income.

From these few studies and the small amount of information available on intrafamily transfers, it is clear that living arrangements provide an important source of economic welfare to aged families (and in some cases an important drain on resources). This component of economic status should be relatively stable over time. However, an additional effect of such pooling of resources could be to stabilize the level of economic welfare of the aged in cases of unusual changes in current resources (or unusual demands on available resources).

NONMARKET ACTIVITIES AND LEISURE TIME

Valuing leisure time and non-market-productive activities for the aged is a difficult task. This subgroup of the population is able to enjoy more hours of leisure and unpaid productive activity than any other age group. If leisure is regarded as a normal good, an increase in its consumption raises the level of economic welfare, ceteris paribus. Consequently, although the level of economic status usually falls when a person retires, at least some of the decrease may be offset by increased consumption of leisure time. The value per unit of leisure to an individual should fall as his or her consumption of leisure time increases. However, the total value of leisure time could still rise. Thus, including non-market-productive activities and leisure in the measure of economic welfare should have a stabilizing influence on the value of $\hat{Y}_t$ over time.

A full income approach to measuring economic welfare attempts to value both unpaid productive activity (such as housework, charity work, and production of goods in the home) and the consumption of leisure time. The appropriate measure for unpaid productive activities is the actual market wage rates for these tasks.[11] However, this approach cannot establish a value for leisure time which is not devoted to such activities. An alternative means for valuing time assumes that, at the margin, the opportunity cost for both unpaid productive activities *and* the consumption of leisure equals foregone earnings in the market (as measured by the after-tax marginal wage rate). This second approach is often simpler and more appropriate for valuing both leisure and nonmarket activities. In fact, a breakdown between these two activities is unnecessary if one assumes, at the margin, equality be-

[11] A more detailed discussion of this approach can be found in Sirageldin (1969).

tween the productivity of leisure and nonmarket activities. Based on the concept of opportunity cost, where hours of leisure time are assumed to be exchanged for hours in the labor force, the rate of commodity substitution of income for leisure equals the after-tax marginal wage rate.[12]

Although this approach to valuing leisure may, in general, be satisfactory, a number of theoretical problems arise when working with aged families. First, a marginal wage rate approach is only appropriate for equilibrium situations. When artificial distortions of the market wage occur, such a measure is invalid. The second problem concerns distortions in the labor–leisure choice of individuals resulting from Social Security and similar retirement schemes. These programs usually alter the slope of the work–leisure possibilities line. Finally, a marginal solution offers no insights into the valuation of inframarginal units of leisure time. Since aged families may spend little time in the work force, this issue is especially important.

Poor health, job discrimination, and mandatory retirement effectively exclude many elderly workers from the labor force. In such cases, an aged worker cannot freely choose his or her leisure at the amount indicated by a tangency between the labor–leisure possibilities line and the individual's indifference curve. For example, if there is sufficient discrimination to prevent his employment, an aged worker may have no rational choice but to retire. Consequently, the value of his leisure time would be lower than the marginal net tax wage rate before retirement. But it is not correct to assume that such an individual places *no* value on leisure time when he or she does not have the option to work. The other important category of aged persons compelled to limit their labor force participation includes those in ill health or with physical limitations resulting from age. For these individuals, the appropriate market wage rate may be zero, but again it is unlikely that this is the appropriate value for their leisure time. Finally, the disequilibrium issue is also clouded because, in practice, there are severe limitations on the availability of data. There is little

[12] The simple analytics can be found in Henderson and Quandt (1958). Their analysis has since been shown to be a special case of a more generalized model which includes the value of time not only in the utility function but also in the production of all goods and services, including those in leisure. That is, leisure should be treated symmetrically with all other commodities. The more restricted notion of the value of leisure is used here for simplicity since the conceptual issues to be discussed would be the same. See, for example, Becker (1965). Sirageldin (1969, pp. 13–17) has expanded this concept even further to include non-market-productive activities in the same fashion as leisure.

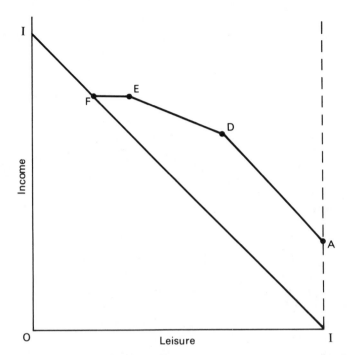

FIGURE 2.1 The effect of Social Security on tradeoffs between income and leisure.

information as to why people retire and whether their choices are voluntary. Moreover, since several factors may be involved in a person's decision to retire, it is probable that the exact mix of voluntary and involuntary reasons would be difficult even for the aged person himself to identify.

The second major source of distortion in valuing leisure time is the retirement incentive from Social Security and other public and private pensions.[13] As illustrated in figure 2.1, before the introduction of a Social Security program, the tradeoff between income and leisure can be shown as line II' with a slope equal to the wage rate net of taxes.[14] The combination of income, hours of leisure, and hours of work is determined by the point of tangency with the individual's indifference curve. An initial Social Security endowment of amount $I'A$ is given to

[13] Related discussions of this issue can be found elsewhere but with the emphasis on the effects of hours at work. See, for example, Pechman, Aaron, and Taussig (1968), and Gallaway (1965).

[14] Since it will subsequently be assumed that II' captures taxes, the qualifying phrase "net of taxes" is omitted. When references to a tax are subsequently made, they will refer to the additional implicit tax resulting from some Social Security scheme.

a fully retired person. The segment DA is a parallel outward shift of the budget line, since Social Security provisions allow an individual to keep up to his first $1,680 in earnings with no reductions. Then for the next $1,200, a 50 percent tax rate is levied against any earnings, causing the slope of DE to be only half the slope of AD. Finally, above $2,880 in earnings the tax rate becomes 100 percent (segment EF), until at point F it is no longer advantageous to receive Social Security benefits.

The value of leisure time for an individual will, at the margin, equal the wage rate only if an indifference curve is tangent to the FI or AD segments of this expanded leisure–income possibilities line. If the tangency occurs between points D and E, leisure at the margin will equal the wage rate net of the earnings tax. The real difficulty in determining the value of leisure under this Social Security scheme arises when tangency occurs at either point E or point D. Since there is a kink in the labor–leisure line at each point, it is not possible to determine the slope of the indifference curve—only a range of values can be identified. Moreover, we must know not only the marginal wage rate and the earnings tax rate but also the size of the Social Security benefit (I'A). If I'A is very large relative to OI, the area where the earnings tax affects the value of leisure will occur closer to full-time employment than if I'A is small relative to OI.

The final obstacle to a marginal wage rate approach is the problem of valuing the inframarginal leisure hours. While economic theory dictates that the last unit of time spent in leisure should be equal to the last unit of time in both market and non-market-productive activities, the inframarginal units need not be. If the demand for leisure time is subject to decreasing marginal utility, the inframarginal units are likely to be valued at more than the estimated value of leisure. The marginal wage rate approach provides only a lower bound on the value of such time. However, the shape of an individual's (or a family's) demand curve would determine the amount by which the value is underestimated. This can vary substantially across families, thus affecting their distributional rankings.

Michael Taussig's (1973, pp. 50–54) research represents one of the few attempts to value leisure for families as part of a measure of economic welfare. He multiplies an estimate of leisure time by the marginal net tax wage rates of individuals. He adjusts leisure time downward for those who are ill or unemployed but makes no attempt to account for involuntary retirement. Although he does impute foregone earnings for those out of the labor force, Taussig does not discuss the methods used. An alternative approach by Morgan (1968) does not attempt to transform leisure into dollar terms. Morgan proposes to measure "enjoyed leisure" and then multiply this figure by a welfare ratio measure of other forms of income (both money and nonmoney). However, as the above discussion points out, it is impossible to separate "enjoyable" from "not enjoyable" leisure, so that in this sense Morgan's measure is of no advantage. This discussion has stressed the importance of the value placed on leisure time by the family. Multiplying hours of "enjoyed" leisure by the welfare ratio effectively weights leisure by the family's ability to enjoy it rather than by the actual value a family places on its leisure time. Thus, many of the conceptual problems discussed above are also included in Morgan's measure.

NET WORTH

In this study, one of the principal deviations from standard treatments of economic welfare is the inclusion of net worth. Measures of economic welfare based on current money income capture only the interest, dividend, and rental payments from the accumulated net worth of a family. However, net worth plays a substantive role in raising the level of well-being of most aged families. Consistent with a life-cycle hypothesis for consumption, the anticipation of lower incomes later in life by the young should cause them to postpone current consumption to ensure security during their retirement years. Consequently, dissaving should provide an important source of well-being to aged families—particularly to those who have retired.[15]

To be consistent with the life-cycle consumption hypothesis, the amount of dissaving in any year should depend upon the size and stability of the other components of economic welfare $(\hat{Y}_t)$. The share of net worth dissaved (S_t) can be adjusted each year to maintain a constant level of potential real consumption over time. For aged families with no labor force participant, $\hat{Y}_t$ would probably show little yearly variation. The largest adjustment in S_t would be required when presently working members of aged families retire. However, public and private retirement programs combined with the value of additional leisure time are likely to provide at least partial earnings replacement, mitigating the size of the adjustment needed in S_t.

---

[15] Even if it is assumed that not all of net worth will be dissaved, the existence of such a stock of wealth is of value to a family no matter how it actually provides utility. The failure to dissave in some "rational" way may imply that *unused* savings are worth more to some families than consumed savings.

An exact figure for the net worth holdings of aged persons is difficult to calculate. Statistics on wealth are rare and there are huge discrepancies among the few available estimates. For example, two separate studies for 1962 listed median assets for the aged at $6,085 and $9,860. The Social Security Administration's lower estimate reflects in part its emphasis on those at the bottom of the distribution. The opposite is true for the higher figure of the Survey of Financial Characteristics of Consumers (Epstein and Murray 1967, pp. 211–13; Projector and Weiss 1966). These methodological biases probably account for only part of the discrepancy. However, even if the more conservative Social Security estimates are employed, net worth still can have an important influence on the economic welfare of aged families.

Findings from the 1968 Social Security Survey of the Aged also highlight two other important aspects of net worth holdings (Murray 1972). First, net assets appear to be increasing over time; the median value rose to about $11,550 in 1967. Net worth holdings are becoming increasingly important to aged families. Second, the large variation in the size of holdings among aged families implies that this component can effect a substantial change in the ranking of families within the distribution.

Burton Weisbrod and W. Lee Hansen (1968) conducted the most important research to date on including net worth in a measure of economic welfare. They asserted that the level of assets owned by an individual enhances his "economic position"—which is simply defined as a function of the flow of services over which the family unit has command. Weisbrod and Hansen maintained only that their approach would improve upon the inequitable, "single-dimensional money income measure" of economic welfare, and did not hail it as an "ideal" or complete indicator. Dorothy Projector and Gertrude Weiss (1969) claimed the Weisbrod–Hansen measure is of only limited value because of the arbitrary method chosen for allocating net worth. In particular, they argued that this bias invalidates the use of the measure to establish eligibility for public programs or to compare across consumer units of different ages. This objection is comparable to arguing that $\hat{Y}_t$ varies over time. Since this study is confined to aged families, the problem is reduced.[16] Moreover, if the assumption that $\hat{Y}_t$ is stable over time is reasonable for aged families, then the Weisbrod–Hansen constant annuity is an appropriate measure for S_t.

---

[16] The Projector–Weiss objection could also be met in a study covering the whole population if attention were given to the stream of earnings expected by families in the future, as was discussed earlier, thus taking into account the ability of younger families to accumulate more wealth over time.

3

The Empirical Measure of
Economic Welfare

The most challenging aspect of this research is the translation of theoretical concepts into empirical measures. Traditionally, empirical problems have been the major deterrent to the development of expanded measures of economic status. Improvements in microdata now allow advances in this area. While many difficulties remain which prevent a fully comprehensive estimate of the theoretical measure, this chapter specifies most of the important components of economic status.[1]

Practical considerations exclude from the measure three sets of variables: certain government expenditures, certain taxes, and the value of leisure time. The theoretical measure of economic welfare (W_t) for an aged family developed in chapter 2 is

$$W_t = (\hat{Y}_t + S_t)\lambda$$
$$\hat{Y}_t = Y_t^e + O_t + G_t + I_t + L_t$$

where

$\hat{Y}_t$ = current nonproperty resources available for consumption in period t

λ = adjustment for family composition

Y_t^e = earned income

---

[1] An earlier version of the empirical measure is summarized in Moon (1976). However, the wage, net worth, tax, and Medicare estimates have all been revised; thus the results presented in chapters 4 and 5 will reflect these substantive changes.

O_t = other private, cash income (excluding property and earned income)

S_t = share of net worth allocated over period t

G_t = the net value of government (including both taxes and expenditures)

I_t = intrafamily transfers

L_t = the value of leisure and non-market-productive activities.

The empirical estimates of earned income, "other" income, and intrafamily transfers pose no obstacles. They are included as described in chapter 2.

However, the value of government expenditures net of taxes must of necessity be less comprehensive than the ideal theoretical specification. G_t consists of four parts, some of which are more readily estimated than others:

$$G_t = G_t^c + G_t^k + G_t^o - T_t$$

where

G_t^c = cash transfers

G_t^k = in-kind transfers

G_t^o = all other direct government expenditures

T_t = total taxes.

Cash transfers are easily identified and incorporated into the measure as part of current money income. The remaining components of government expenditures pose complicated problems. Only those in-kind transfers (G_t^{k*})—Medicare, Medicaid, and public housing—for which recipients can be identified are included. Similarly, taxes (T_t^*) are limited to federal personal and payroll taxes. These transfers and taxes can be calculated separately for each family from available data. Finally, since a reasonable measure of the value of direct government expenditures to aged families would itself be a major undertaking, no attempt is made to estimate this portion of government's impact. No established measures of the incidence of these expenditures are available to calculate their contribution to a family's well-being.

The final component of $\hat{Y}_t$, the value of leisure time and non-market-productive activities (L_t), is not estimated. As discussed in chapter 2, there are a number of conceptual problems involved in valuing these commodities in dollar terms. Moreover, the actual estimation of the value of leisure would require substantive information on the reasons for lack of labor force participation by aged persons—data which are unavailable. Any attempt to calculate crudely the value of leisure would be unable to capture substantive differences among families.

The estimated share of net worth (S_t^*) also differs from the theoretical discussion of that component in chapter 2. Y_t^* cannot be predicted accurately over the remaining lifetime of the family; as yet we still have too little information in this area. Thus, S_t^* will, with one exception, be held constant. A one-time adjustment is calculated for S_t^* to reflect the withdrawal of aged family members from the labor force. This is undoubtedly the largest single change that occurs in $\hat{Y}_t$ for aged families.

Thus, the empirical measure of economic welfare, with appropriate modifications, is the following:

$$W_t^* = (Y_t^* + S_t^*)\lambda$$
$$Y_t^* = Y_t^e + O_t + G_t^c + G_t^{k*} - T_t^* + I_t.$$

The asterisks identify components included but which do not exactly correspond to the theoretical specification. Following a brief description of the data source used, the precise estimation procedures for each of these components are discussed below.

THE SURVEY OF ECONOMIC OPPORTUNITY

The basic source of data for this research is the Survey of Economic Opportunity (SEO). The Bureau of the Census conducted this survey for the Office of Economic Opportunity in 1966 and 1967 for the years 1965 and 1966. It sampled over 30,000 households nationwide. This research uses over 6,100 interview units with at least one member aged sixty-five and older.[2] More than 7,000 aged individuals are thus included. Size is the SEO's major advantage. Moreover, it contains information on assets and family income divided by source— attributes which are necessary for the development of the expanded

---

[2] An interview unit consists of all persons residing in the same household who are related to each other by blood, marriage, or adoption. This does not necessarily correspond to the definition for family used in this research (as described in chapter 2). The SEO provides a weighting scheme to yield population estimates. The decomposition of extended families into two parts—the young and the old—causes some potential problems in using the SEO weights. However, in no case are families double-counted. This technique allows the establishment of only one aged nuclear family. While the analysis utilizes information about the younger component of an extended unit, it is never counted as a separate family. This should reduce any bias in the nationally weighted estimates. Indeed, the characteristics of the aged sample correspond well with other demographic breakdowns for this group.

measure of economic status. The SEO's major disadvantage is its date; however, no later microdata source available is as complete.

STANDARDIZING BY FAMILY SIZE

Although about two-thirds of all aged persons reside in one- or two-member families, family size for the aged can vary substantially. Therefore, a means of comparing across family size is essential for deriving a measure of well-being for elderly families. Families with equal resources but of different size are not equally well-off. This research employs two different, although related, schemes for standardizing the distribution. The first, a welfare ratio measure, is common in many distributional studies.[3] The actual resources of a family are divided by a standardized set of budget needs determined by the size and composition of the family. A welfare ratio of "one" indicates that the family's resources just coincide with its "needs."

The second adjustment for family size and composition converts income or economic welfare to "equivalency units." Expressed in dollar terms, this measure converts the measured resources of a unit into the number of dollars necessary for a standardized family (an aged couple, for example) to achieve a comparable level of economic welfare. The dollar amount of economic welfare of a large aged family is consequently scaled down while the welfare level of a family composed of a single individual is boosted. The following formula, based on the ith family's welfare (W_i), calculates this equivalency measure (F_i):

$$F_i = W_i/(p_i/\bar{p})$$

where
$\bar{p}$ = poverty threshold for some standard unit
p_i = poverty threshold for the ith family.

With either of these adjustments, one distribution summarizes the economic welfare of aged families of any size.

CASH COMPONENTS OF ECONOMIC WELFARE

Private Cash Components

Three elements of economic status—earnings of aged family members, private pensions, and "other" income—constitute the pri-

[3] See David (1959).

vate cash components.[4] If property income were included, the private portion of money income would be complete. For the most part, the distribution of these components comes directly from SEO data, with adjustments necessary for only those interview units which form an extended family group. The SEO lists earnings separately for each person. Private pensions are assumed to accrue solely to the aged subfamily when the interview unit consists of a larger extended family. Thus, the "other" income category net of private pensions is the only component which must be arbitrarily divided between the aged and young subfamilies. In general, "other" income is small in amount and limited in scope, so that whatever method the researcher uses, any bias in the distribution of economic welfare is minimal. This study allocates a share of "other" income to each subfamily in proportion to its size relative to total family size.

It is, however, necessary to adjust current earnings for inclusion in the measure of economic status. If cash income from wages and salaries (earnings) were simply added to the expanded measure, it would, in general, bias upward the level of economic status for those aged families with at least one labor force participant. Unless that worker remains active for the rest of his or her life, or unless pensions or other resources totally replace lost income from this source upon retirement, Y_t^* will fall when someone in the family retires. Rather than making two separate annuity calculations, the adjustment is generated through a reduction in the amount of current earnings treated as permanent income; only that portion replaced by other sources is included. That is, Social Security and other retirement benefits will partially replace lost earnings. The remainder (viewed as transitory income) is added to net worth to be incorporated into the annuity. By spreading this transitory portion of earnings across the family's lifetime, the share of net worth implicitly increases to compensate for earnings lost upon the retirement of the worker(s) If any individual plans to work, say, for one-third of his or her remaining lifetime, then only about one-third of current earnings actually contributes to current potential consumption. The remainder must be saved for consumption after retirement. Unfortunately, there are no data to forecast how much longer labor force participants will continue to work. Consequently, I make three hypothetical calculations of future earned income: an in-

---

[4] "Other" income is a catchall category which includes private sources of current income other than earnings and returns to assets. For example, private monetary transfers to or from persons outside the household are contained in this measure, along with royalties and annuities. Private pensions, which are also part of "other" income, are discussed separately here because they can be assigned to the aged family by a different set of assumptions.

termediate solution falling between estimated upper and lower bounds.

The intermediate approach assumes that aged workers will retire, but not immediately. I arbitrarily assume that an aged person currently in the labor force will remain so until reaching age seventy or for two more years, whichever is longer. This breakdown approximately corresponds to one-third of each aged person's life expectancy. Figures from the 1968 Survey of the Aged suggest that the labor force remains a fairly constant fraction for aged persons from age sixty-five to age seventy (Bixby et al. 1975, p. 93). While any person over sixty-five is unlikely to continue working until age seventy, this is not as unlikely for the individual who remains in the labor force at age sixty-five.

Social Security and other public and private transfer programs replace a portion of earnings lost by a retiring aged worker. Consequently, that particular portion is added directly to the measure of economic status. Net worth–annuity calculations include the remainder. The Social Security benefit formula for 1967 forms the basis for the income replacement estimate. The calculated potential benefit for each aged worker—and, if appropriate, his or her dependents—assumes that income listed in the survey year is representative of average wages. In actuality, wages and salaries in that year may be atypical, and some aged workers will receive additional private pensions that go unmeasured. The bias from the procedure outlined here probably results in an understatement of potential income replacement, although for many aged persons in 1966, Social Security constituted their only pension program.

The remainder, after subtracting replacement (permanent) income, is multiplied by the estimated number of years the individual will remain in the labor force. Next, this remainder is added to net worth to be included in the annuity. This technique implicitly results in a smaller annuity during the working years, increasing at retirement to just compensate for the reduction in current income.

The upper bound solution, yielding the highest level of economic status, incorporates earnings directly into the welfare measure rather than through the annuity calculation. This is comparable to assuming that all aged workers remain in the labor force until death, or that public and private pension programs totally compensate for lost earnings. The lower bound assumes that all aged labor force participants retire in the year following the survey. Consequently, the current year's earnings, over and above expected increases in pension or other transfer programs, are treated as transitory income and added to net worth to be allocated over the family's remaining "lifetime." This procedure lowers the measure of economic status for families whose earnings comprise an important share of current income, since much of this one year's earned income is spread across the remaining years of life expectancy.

Public Cash Transfers

The SEO provides data for government cash transfers. The transfers included are (1) Social Security and Railroad Retirement, (2) government employees' pensions, (3) veterans' benefits, (4) unemployment insurance and workmen's compensation, and (5) public assistance. The SEO lists these transfers as part of total family income. Consequently, when it is necessary to allocate these sources among members of an extended family, the first two transfers are assumed to accrue solely to the aged subfamily. The allocation procedure for veterans' benefits, unemployment insurance, workmen's compensation, and public assistance is the same as for "other" income. The aged subfamily's proportion is the ratio of aged family size to total unit size. As with "other" income, this allocation of veterans' benefits, workmen's compensation, and unemployment insurance should not greatly affect the level of economic welfare since these are small programs. Moreover, the sharing of income should be a reasonable assumption in the case of public assistance, where benefits are generally granted to the family as a whole rather than to separate members.

NET WORTH

At any point in time, the net worth of a family represents a stock of wealth. The measure of economic welfare requires a current flow of resources representing a yearly depletion of wealth by an aged family. If Y_t^* is stable over time and a constant level of consumption is desired, a constant annuity formula correctly converts net worth into a flow. For the empirical estimates the only variation allowed in non-property resources (Y_t^*) is a one-time adjustment when an aged worker retires. However, rather than making two separate annuity calculations, the adjustment occurs through a reduction in the amount of current earnings contained in Y_t^*; only that portion which would be replaced by other sources is included. The annuity calculation captures the remainder and thus spreads this transitory portion of earnings across the family's lifetime. The share of net worth (S_t^*) implicitly increases to compensate for lost earnings upon the retirement of the worker(s).

Thus, a standard annuity formula, based on an average of the expected lifetime of the family's members and the rate of return on assets, best reflects the share of net worth (S_t^*):[5]

$$S_t^* = A \left(\frac{r}{1 - (1 + r)^{-N}} \right)$$

where

S_t^* = annual estimated share of net worth
A = net worth at the beginning of period t
r = real rate of return on assets
N = life expectancy in years.

Net worth includes all assets minus all debts reported by each family. Home equity is incorporated in an adjusted form. Where appropriate, A also contains the transitory portion of earned income.

Life expectancy estimates vary by the age and sex of individuals. When an elderly family has more than one member—a couple or several related aged persons—N is a composite figure based on an average of the life expectancy estimates for each family member.[6] The interest rate (r) should reflect some real rate of return on assets for the aged. The 2 percent estimate used here represents the low rate an aged family purchasing such an annuity could expect.

The SEO net worth information is missing or unusable for about 24 percent of all aged families. This certainly poses formidable problems and casts some doubt on the value of the remaining net worth data. Nonetheless, the SEO remains one of the most reliable sources for these data. Moreover, the available data provide a basis for estimating the missing values. To impute a value for net worth for each of the families without data, this research used a linear regression model which predicts net worth from socioeconomic variables of those families whose records are intact. While this estimation procedure is unbiased around the mean, it artificially reduces the variance of the imputed values. Consequently, the estimates derived here are treated to a random shock to increase their variance to the same level as the

---

[5] This is similar to the approach used in Weisbrod and Hansen (1968).

[6] An alternative approach (used by Weisbrod and Hansen) allows for a reduced annuity for the surviving member when one spouse dies. The life expectancy figures are based on U.S. Public Health Service (1971).

variance for available net worth data. (See Appendix A for a more complete discussion.)

Since the SEO does not list assets and debts by each subfamily or individual, there is no way to directly allocate "ownership" when aged persons reside in larger extended families. It is assumed that net worth "belongs" to the head of the family. If the head of such a family is under sixty-five and not the spouse of an aged person, net worth for the elderly subfamily is constrained to be zero. In general, the person designated as head of the family is more likely to be in a better financial position and therefore in control of the family's assets. For example, a survey of Wisconsin's aged families indicated that 96 percent of all homeowners are listed as head or spouse of household head, suggesting the close correspondence between home-ownership by an aged unit and the designation of an aged person as the family head (Wisconsin, Dept. of Health and Social Services 1971). Steiner and Dorfman (1957) also found a relationship between the designation of an aged member of an extended family as the head and the income level of the aged subfamily. Median income for the aged unit is higher when the head of the extended family is over sixty-five. However, Steiner and Dorfman cautioned that some bias exists from the honorific designation of an aged member as family head when in actuality the elderly person might be dependent upon younger relatives. To the extent that this bias also exists for the SEO data, some asset income is incorrectly assigned to aged subfamilies. However, at a later point in the measure of economic welfare, the allocation of intrafamily transfers results in a sharing of this net worth among the members of the extended family. These transfers substantially reduce any bias from incorrectly attributing net worth to the family head, since other family members also receive a portion of net worth.

Home Equity

An aged family is generally unable to ration the flow of housing services over its lifetime so as to just exhaust the full measure of value. Unless a house is sold—thus precluding future housing services from that unit—an aged owner does not reap total benefits from the house. Consequently, the value of home equity included in net worth is adjusted downward. The resulting value reflects what a private individual would receive for the sale of his home in exchange for a current annuity, with the purchaser not assuming control of the house until the death of the surviving spouse.

The value of a home should represent the capitalized value of the flow of housing services (rental services) it provides over its "lifetime":

$$H = \sum_{t=t_0}^{D} \frac{R_t}{(1 + v)^t}$$

where

H = value of home to the owner
t_0 = the present time
D = expected life of the home in years
R_t = rental value of services in period t
v = rate of time preference.

Moreover, the value of the home to the aged owner can be further subdivided into the value of the housing services the homeowner receives during his lifetime and the "salable" value of the home at his death. This latter portion consists of the capitalized value of services from death of the owner for the remaining life of the house:

$$H = \sum_{t=t_0}^{N} \frac{R_t}{(1 + v)^t} + \sum^{D} \frac{R_t}{(1 + v)^t}$$

where

N = years of life expectancy of the aged person (or his surviving spouse, whichever is longer).

The first portion of the above equation represents a lifetime in-kind annuity. The second part could hypothetically be sold to, say, an insurance company in exchange for a lifetime cash annuity. The aged person (and spouse) would reside in the house rent free until the death of the surviving member, at which time the insurance company would receive title to the property. Thus, the aged family would be able to recoup at least some of the value of the home which results from housing services provided after the death of the family members.[7] The process may be informally approached when adult children care for their aged parent(s) presently with the expectation of inheriting an estate.

The value of this "salable" portion of the asset—as perceived by the insurance company—is

$$\sum_{t=N}^{D} \frac{R_t}{(1 + z)^t}$$

[7] A similar "actuarial mortgage plan" has been suggested by Yung-Ping Chen (1967) as a possible way for the government to aid in converting assets into cash for the aged.

where

z = discount rate of the insurance company.

The percentage z should include the risks involved in deferring receipt of the asset until the death of the homeowner and a normal return to the insurance company. Therefore, z will be larger than the owner's rate of time preference (v). The larger is z, the smaller is the present value of the "salable" portion of the home. Thus, the insurance company would effectively base its annuity payments on a lower principal. The amount of the reduction in the value of the home can be expressed as:

$$J = \sum_{t=N}^{D} \frac{R_t}{(1 + v)^t} - \sum_{t=N}^{D} \frac{R_t}{(1 + z)^t}.$$

Before home equity can be converted into an annuity, it must be adjusted downward to reflect the lower value of the "salable" portion of the home.

The following table gives an indication of the effects of the crucial variables $(v, z, N,$ and $D)$ on the magnitude of the reduction. For simplicity, R_t is assumed to remain constant over time. Table 3.1 lists pairs of variables v and z and N and D in several combinations to illustrate the effects of both the spread of the differences $(D - N$ and $z - v)$ and the actual value of the variables. For example, the number of percentage points difference between the interest rates, v and z, is the most important aspect of that relationship, although the effect of a particular spread is altered slightly depending upon whether v is set at, say, 4 percent or 6 percent.

TABLE 3.1
Reduction in Home Value in Response to Combinations of v, z, N, D
(Expressed as Percentages of Total Value)

Combinations of N and D	Combinations of v and z		
	4% and 10%	6% and 12%	6% and 16%
10 and 15	13.3 %	12.27%	16.58%
15 and 20	11.2	9.58	12.24
10 and 20	22.1	19.97	26.28
15 and 25	18.9	15.95	19.94

NOTE: v = rate of time preference.
z = discount rate of the insurance company.
N = life expectancy of the aged person (or his surviving spouse, whichever is longer).
D = life expectancy of the home in years.

A similar relationship holds for the difference between the life expectancy of the house *(D)* and the life expectancy of the homeowner *(N)*. The important issue is how long the home will last after the owner's death (and hence be in the hands of the insurance company). The longer this period, the greater the reduction in value. To obtain the reduction as a percentage of the total value of the home, the size of the difference *(D − N)* in relation to the total life expectancy of the house [i.e., *(D − N)/D*] must also be known. If *D* is large relative to *(D − N)*, then the owner enjoys a greater share of the value of the home in the form of housing services, and the portion of the value annuitized—the salable portion—is relatively small. The first two rows of table 3.1 illustrate this effect. In the first case, the five-year difference *(D − N)* reflects one-third of total *D*. In the second case, where *D* is twenty years, the difference represents only one-fourth of the life expectancy of the home. As a result there is a smaller reduction in home value, given the interest rates.

Unfortunately, neither R_t nor *D* are known, and hence the reduction in home value can only be estimated indirectly, as a percentage of total value *(H)*. The small amount of available information on the age of homes owned by persons over sixty-five suggests that the older the person, the older the home.[8] This coincides with the observation that many aged persons who own a home lived in the same residence during their working years. If these cursory observations are correct, then *(D − N)* may be relatively constant across most people. Consequently, the fraction *(D − N)/D* would vary only with differences in the life expectancy of the surviving person *(N)*.[9] Although this additional assumption would strengthen the relationship, nonetheless the longer the life expectancy of the homeowner, the greater the percentage of the life of the home which yields housing services to the owner, and hence the smaller the reduction in total value.

Consequently, the estimated insurance reduction *(J*)* is a function of the homeowner's life expectancy:

$$J^* = \left(\frac{B}{B + N} \right) cH$$

where

B = some constant representing *(D − N)*
c = a percentage representing some combination of *v* and *z*
H = total value of the home.

---

[8] See, for example, Wisconsin Dept. of Health and Social Services (1971).

[9] For example, if *(D − N)* is constant at ten years, when *N* also equals ten years, the fraction must be one-half. When *N* is fifteen years, the fraction would be two-fifths.

B is set at ten years and at 60 percent. These values provide substantial reductions in the amount of home equity included in the annuity. When life expectancy is ten years, J^* provides a 30 percent reduction in home equity.[10]

IN-KIND TRANSFERS

In-kind programs included in this research are the important medical transfer programs, Medicare and Medicaid, and public housing. Other transfers were excluded because of difficulties in identifying recipients. However, in 1967, these other transfers were small in size and would not have appreciably altered the distribution of economic welfare. As recently as 1971 other in-kind programs, including food stamps, totaled only $163 million for the aged (U.S., Bureau of the Budget 1972, p. 191).

Medicare

The Medicare program was enacted as Title XVIII of the Social Security Amendments of 1965 to provide greater access to health care by aged persons. There are two different sections of the provision, one designed primarily for Social Security beneficiaries and the other open to anyone over sixty-five. Part A provides hospital insurance financed by Social Security payroll taxes to eligible beneficiaries. Part B, the smaller portion, is a voluntary program allowing anyone over sixty-five to purchase insurance for physicians' services at reduced rates. Termed "Supplementary Medical Insurance," Part B had an enrollment of 19.6 million aged persons in 1970, while 20.4 million—representing almost universal coverage—were enrolled in Part A (Schultze et al. 1972, p. 220).

Medicare is most appropriately viewed as a health insurance program for persons over sixty-five. Benefits equal the amount of the insurance premium subsidized by the government allocated to all persons *eligible* to receive payments. It is assumed that the eligible population consists of all persons over sixty-five, although in actuality about 4 percent of the aged are not covered by either Part A or Part B of Medicare. Treating Medicare as an insurance program avoids the problem of overestimating the well-being of those in ill health. That is,

[10] This amount is greater than any of the reductions shown in table 3.1. Hence, this reduction provides a conservative estimate of home equity. This may also help to prevent the overstatement of benefits to aged families who continue to reside in homes that exceed their needs.

if benefits were allocated according to actual payments received, the more medical bills incurred by an individual, the better off that individual would appear to be. Certainly, most persons consider themselves less well-off when they are ill. Moreover, since some medical costs must still be borne by the individuals, their burdens rise even though Medicare benefits increase. Thus, an aged person receiving Medicare benefits is likely, ceteris paribus, to be less well-off than his healthy counterpart.

The per capita insurance benefit for Medicare is computed for each census region by dividing payments plus administrative costs of the program by the number of persons eligible. From this gross insurance benefit, the premium required for enrollment in Part B is subtracted. Therefore, net benefits are

$$MR_j = (V_j + X_j)/K_j - Q$$

where

MR_j = net insurance benefit for each region j
V_j = amount of vendor payments under Medicare in each region
X_j = administrative costs for each region
K_j = number of aged persons in the region
Q = individual's contribution to Part B insurance.

The inclusion of vendor payments and administrative costs in the calculations results in a lower-bound estimate of what individuals would have to pay to receive such insurance through the private market. For fiscal 1967, the cost of enrolling in Part B was $36 per year and is deducted as the private contribution to the cost of the insurance.[11]

Although Medicare is a national program, Feldstein (1971) has found that Medicare benefits vary widely across states. Feldstein developed an econometric model based on demographic and economic characteristics of local health care systems. Differences in the demand for medical services and in the available supply explain substantial portions of the variations in benefits. As a consequence, Feldstein concluded that Medicare does not provide equal insurance benefits to all aged persons. Rather, the value of the insurance benefit

---

[11] However, a number of aged persons did not even have to pay this amount, since their private contributions were paid by Medicaid funds. States have the option of "buying into" the Medicare program to provide insurance coverage for those aged who are eligible for Title XIX (Medicaid) benefits. Nonetheless, the private insurance contribution is subtracted from gross insurance benefits since the benefits to individuals from this "buy in" procedure are captured in Medicaid benefits.

should be computed for the state in which the aged beneficiaries reside. To the extent that these differences also reflect price level variations, they should be adjusted to obtain the real insurance values to aged persons.[12] Since the SEO data preclude a statewide breakdown, regional insurance values have been imputed instead.[13]

Although this regional breakdown captures important differences in access to Medicare benefits, a number of other variables are equally important. Within each region, reimbursement per eligible recipient varies substantially by such characteristics as urban versus rural location, income, race, and sex.[14] Some of these differences reflect personal preferences or the overall health status of the group. However, when these characteristics capture differential access to health care, the insurance values should be adjusted to reflect the lower (or higher) probability of receiving medical services.

Urban versus rural location is likely to reflect probability differences, since the number and quality of facilities and physicians differ substantially by place of residence. Second, higher income individuals are able to utilize more services—both quantitatively and qualitatively—by having better transportation and information about medical care. In these cases, health status may also vary, but with the bias toward greater needs for lower income families. Thus, the greater utilization of Medicare by upper income families underscores the importance of factors other than health status. Finally, substantial differences in utilization by race also suggest limited access for and perhaps discrimination against nonwhites in receiving medical care.

Ideally, the marginal adjustments to the insurance value for each characteristic should hold health status and all other variables constant. Then, with the same techniques as those used for the regional insurance values, benefits could be computed within each region from the aged person's demographic and socioeconomic characteristics. However, because of data limitations and the problems from dividing the sample into numerous small cells, only one set of additional adjustments is feasible. Within each region, Medicare insurance benefits vary by family income class but not by race or urban–rural location.[15]

---

[12] No specific price level adjustments are made here since such estimates are difficult to obtain for medical care by region. While this tends to exaggerate the differences somewhat, significant variations would remain even if price differences were taken into account.

[13] These estimates were derived from data contained in Stuart (1971).

[14] See, for example, Davis and Reynolds (1973).

[15] These estimates were calculated from unpublished data of the Current Medicare Survey for 1968. As a result of a large underreporting problem, there may be some bias in the results. Consequently, only four broad income classes are used.

TABLE 3.2

Medicare Insurance Benefits by Income and Region of Residence, 1967

Income Class	Region			
	Northeast	North Central	South	West
Under $5000	$187.67	$166.30	$131.00	$229.48
$5000–9999	200.87	177.99	140.21	245.61
$10,000–14,999	274.72	243.44	191.76	335.92
$15,000 or more	383.28	339.64	267.49	468.67

SOURCE: Derived from Stuart (1971) and unpublished data from Current Medicare Survey.

The adjustment divides the amount of benefits going to each broad income class within the region by the number of aged recipients in that income category. Table 3.2 shows the results of these adjustments. Per capita insurance benefits range from the $131 received by low-income aged families in the South to benefits of $468.67 for high-income aged families in the West.

Benefits are added to the measure of economic welfare according to region of residence and number of persons over sixty-five within the family. Since these are per capita yearly benefits, family benefits simply equal the number of aged persons in the family multiplied by the appropriate insurance amount and then adjusted by the family size standardization described earlier.

Medicaid

The Medicaid program under Title XIX of the Social Security Amendments of 1965 provides medical care to needy persons of all ages. In 1969, more than 3 million persons over age sixty-five received benefits totaling $1.8 billion. This amount represents more than 40 percent of all Medicaid vendor payments for 1969 (U.S., Dept. of Health, Education and Welfare 1972). Benefits and eligibility vary dramatically across the country because Medicaid programs depend upon state participation. Matching grants from the federal government pay 50 to 83 percent of program costs for each state. If a state decides to participate, it must meet certain minimum standards on services and coverage provided. In addition, the federal government matches a broad range of extras. Thus, the size of the benefits varies even among participating states since the comprehensiveness of the program is not fixed. One of the most important sources of variation for the aged is the inclusion (or exclusion) of nursing home care under Medicaid.

Any aged person receiving Supplemental Security Income (SSI)— or in 1967, Old Age Assistance (OAA) or other federal assistance programs—must be covered under each state Medicaid scheme. At the option of the state, the federal grant can also cover "medically indigent" persons. This group generally comprises people above the income limits for assistance whose incomes cannot absorb the drain of large medical expenses. This allows an even wider range of coverage: in fiscal 1968, thirteen states and the District of Columbia had no Medicaid programs. Benefits for the thirty-seven remaining states varied widely, with twenty-three having provisions for the "medically indigent" (O'Connor 1971).

However, absence of a Medicaid program in 1968 should not be interpreted as indicating a complete lack of medical benefits for the aged in a particular state. The 1960 Kerr–Mills provisions for Medical Assistance for the Aged (MAA) allowed generous federal matching grants to states to provide for medically needy aged persons. In addition, many states provided some care through public assistance programs. While the 1965 Social Security Amendments were designed to replace other programs, states had the option of retaining those other programs until the end of 1969. A number of states did retain their MAA and public assistance medical programs (Commerce Clearing House 1968). In fact, in some states MAA expenditures provided higher benefits for those over sixty-five than did states with Medicaid coverage (U.S., Dept. of Health, Education and Welfare 1967).[16] As a consequence, this study does not restrict itself to Medicaid but also includes these substitute programs.

Medicaid provides an insurance scheme in which benefits accrue to all *eligible* persons in the form of subsidized insurance premiums. For the aged, eligibility for public assistance payments is likely to be very stable, since the income positions of most poor and near-poor aged families will, at best, remain constant over time. Thus, if an aged family or individual resides in a state with Medicaid and qualifies for the program, receipt of benefits depends only upon someone in the family becoming ill. As with Medicare, treating Medicaid as insurance

---

[16] For example, Nebraska and Colorado are listed as each having 177,000 persons over sixty-five in 1967. Nebraska, a Medicaid state, expended $6 million on vendor payments for the aged during the first half of calendar 1967 as compared to Colorado's $9 million provided through MAA (U.S., Dept. of Health, Education and Welfare [1967]).

avoids the problem of overstating the well-being of people suffering from poor health or disabilities.

The insurance value of Medicaid *(MC)* to each aged person is estimated as follows for each region and type of program:

$$MC_{ej} = V_{ej}(1 + x)/E_{ej}$$

where

V_{ej} = payment to individuals in the *ej*th recipient class
e = 1 if person receives public assistance or 2 if person qualifies as medically indigent
j = region of residence of recipient
x = administrative costs of the program as a fraction of V
E_{ej} = number of eligible persons per class for each *e* and *j*.

Administrative costs *(x)* are added as a fraction of benefit payments. These costs totaled 4.7 percent of payments in 1967 (U.S., Bureau of the Census 1970, pp. 297–300). It is assumed that administrative costs are equally distributed among regions and types of Medicaid recipients, so that *x* is always 4.7 percent for any insurance class. The ideal measure for place of residence is by state, since payments and eligibility are standardized on that level. However, as mentioned above, families on the SEO can only be identified by census region. As a consequence, these four regions—Northeast, North Central, West, and South—represent the *j*s in this research.

Besides distinguishing beneficiaries by region, this formula treats the aged already on assistance separately from those classified as "medically indigent."[17] Benefits to these two groups within the same region differ. In fiscal 1969, the average Medicaid vendor payment was $252 for persons also receiving money assistance payments and $387 for the medically indigent (U.S., Dept. of Health, Education, and Welfare 1972). The variation in payments reflects the nature of the Medicaid program for these two groups. Medicaid pays a wide range of medical bills for public assistance recipients, including even small bills. On the other hand, Medicaid for the medically needy helps soften the blow of major medical expenses that families close to the poverty line cannot afford. The size of the benefits for these two pro-

---

[17] In addition to these adjustments, there are also differences in access to the Medicaid program by the demographic characteristics of recipient families. As was the case with Medicare, urban–rural residence and race are among the most important. A more complete analysis should calculate differential insurance benefits on the basis of these characteristics. For more discussion on how these variables affect Medicaid, see Holahan (1975).

grams is usually reversed when Medicaid is treated as an insurance program. The number of persons receiving OAA is considerably smaller than the number eligible under the medically needy category, so that when benefits are divided among the eligible population, the insurance amounts are larger for the OAA recipients.

Since payments under Medicaid vary both by region (j) and by "type" of eligibility (e), MC is computed separately for each e and j, resulting in eight different insurance values. The first step in disaggregating these payments by type of eligibility is to determine the proportion of each state's payments devoted to "welfare" and "indigent" groups.[18] Once the benefits are allocated between the two "types" of coverage, payments for each region equal the sum of payments of each type for the states in the region.

The number of persons eligible for Medicaid under the welfare recipient category (E_{1j}) equals the number of people in aged families receiving Old Age Assistance in region j. For the medically needy category, E_{2j} contains all aged families that are below the appropriate income and asset limits established for each region j but who do not receive OAA.[19] Each state establishes its own income and asset limits. Consequently these limits vary considerably.[20] The income limits for each region $(\overline{Y}_j)$ equal an average of the states' limits weighted by the aged population of each state:

$$\overline{Y}_j = \sum_s (K_{sj}/K_j)\overline{Y}_{sj}$$

[18] Information on the proportion of payments made to recipients of public assistance is available only for Medicaid payments to the population as a whole. Therefore, it is assumed that OAA recipients in a state receive approximately the same percentage of all benefits granted to persons over sixty-five as the overall public assistance percentage of total Medicaid payments in each state.

[19] Technically, persons with higher incomes may also receive these benefits. Very large medical bills which effectively drive income and assets below the appropriate limits may qualify a family for some medical aid. However, there is no way of identifying how often this occurs. Therefore this study will follow the implicit assumption contained in the research of both O'Connor and Stuart and ignore the potential eligibilities of higher income groups. Information on the asset limits for public assistance in states with no "medically indigent" provision are obtained by averaging the limits given for states with such programs.

[20] While some states do not provide for the medically needy, almost all give some benefits to persons not on public assistance. These persons often have incomes that would make them eligible for aid but for some other reason are not receiving cash assistance. Also, MAA provisions do not require that recipients receive OAA, so these states provide aid to a loosely defined "medically needy" category. Therefore, income limits in states without "medically needy" provisions are set equal to the income limits for public assistance in those states.

TABLE 3.3
Insurance Benefits to Public Assistance Recipients by Region of Residence, 1967

Region	Number of OAA Recipients in 1967	Total Benefits	Benefits per OAA Recipient
South	1,206,900	$170,646,028	$141.39
West	407,700	198,666,575	487.28
Northeast	268,600	151,625,598	564.50
North Central	359,600	172,482,152	479.65
U.S.	2,242,800	$693,420,353	$309.18

SOURCE: Derived from U.S., Dept. of Health, Education and Welfare (1967).

where

$\overline{Y}_j$ = income limit in region j
$\overline{Y}_{sj}$ = income limit for each state s in the region
K_{sj} = number of persons over sixty-five in state s of region j
K_j = total number of persons over sixty-five in region j.

Table 3.3 lists the insurance values for public assistance recipients in each region (MC_{1j}). The number of adults in the aged family determines the allocation of the per capita benefits.[21] There results a substantial regional variation in benefits, ranging from $141.39 per recipient in the South to $564.50 per recipient in the Northeast. Because of the large number of OAA recipients in the South, the national average is only $309.18. Total benefits as computed are less than actual benefits because of missing or unusable data.[22] The information in table 3.4 refers to benefits for medically needy recipients. Again there is variation among regions, but the variation between the South and all other regions is the largest.

Public Housing

In 1971, 332,000 people over age sixty-five (or in families headed by an aged person) received some form of direct housing benefits from the federal government. Public housing in the United States exists in several forms. The major type is low-rent housing provided through publicly owned housing projects, as established by the Housing Act of

[21] When there are children present in an aged family, benefits are allocated to them but at insurance values computed for AFDC (Aid for Dependent Children) children (or for the medically needy, for the number of eligible children). These values are listed in Appendix B.
[22] Data were missing for four states: Alaska, Maine, Nevada, and North Carolina. Consequently, computation of the insurance values disregards these states.

TABLE 3.4
Medicaid Insurance Benefits to the Medically Needy by Region of Residence, 1967

				Benefits	
Region	Income Limits*	Asset Limits*	Number Eligible	Total	Per Recipient
South	$1720	$1238	619,071	$ 49,107,755	$ 79.32
West	2788	1400	292,648	82,283,730	281.17
Northeast	3190	3228	1,266,665	312,258,222	246.52
North Central	2294	1557	819,830	184,929,097	225.57
U.S.			2,998,214	$628,587,804	$209.65

SOURCE: Derived from U.S., Dept. of Health, Education and Welfare (1967).
* Income and asset limits listed are for an aged couple.

1937. In addition, some benefits are provided through rent supplements and aid to low income homeowners (U.S., Bureau of the Budget 1972, p. 191). However, this research presumes that public housing recipients are those who reside in public housing units. Although these housing programs subsidize less than 2 percent of the aged, this transfer provides substantial benefits to the individual recipient. Including housing programs in the measure should have little effect on the total distribution. It will, however, be of interest later to examine beneficiaries by level of economic welfare.

Two steps are necessary to obtain public housing benefits. First, matching data from the 1966 SEO, which contains information on public housing, to the 1967 tape allows the identification of recipients. The 1967 survey consists of reinterviewed households from the 1966 sample. Thus, the cross-year match indicates whether a family received public housing benefits. Although there is a small identification problem when families moved or were not reinterviewed in 1967, it does not affect the distributions.

The problem of valuing benefits received has no easy solution. If the subsidy is calculated from the tenant's point of view, then the benefit is the money value of the utility placed on the housing minus the rent the family pays. Since participation in public housing is voluntary, there is presumably a positive subsidy to the tenants. It may not, however, be as high as either the costs of providing that housing (over and above the rent paid) or the difference between the market rental value and rent actually paid. As Smolensky and Gomery (1973) have pointed out, the costs of providing public housing are high compared to the market value of a particular unit. Therefore, the subsidy is more reasonably valued against the market rent of a comparable unit in the

private sector, since the tenant's valuation cannot be feasibly estimated here. This study uses the Smolensky–Gomery method to calculate a market value of public housing units.

In 1967 the statutory provisions for public housing established
that units could rent for no more than 80 percent of market value and
cost tenants no more than 20 percent of their income. From these
figures a proxy for market value can be obtained. If

$$R_b{}^* = .8M_b \qquad \text{and} \qquad R_b{}^* = .2\overline{Y}_b$$

then

$$M_b = .25\overline{Y}_b$$

where

$R_b{}^* =$ the maximum rent for tenant b
$M_b =$ the market value of the tenant's housing unit
$\overline{Y}_b =$ the applicable income limit for tenant b.

Consequently, for families of the same size residing in the same region, market value is assumed to equal 25 percent of the upper income
limit for that group. The housing subsidy *(PH)* for each family therefore is

$$PH_b = .25\overline{Y}_b - R_b$$

where

$R_b =$ actual rent paid.

Such a calculation ensures those with incomes considerably below the
public housing income limit a higher subsidy than those families close
to the limit.[23]

TAXES

This study examines the distributional effects of two sets of taxes:
the federal personal income tax and the Social Security payroll tax. For
the remaining federal, state, and local taxes, several tactics are possi-

[23] Of course, this assumes that rents actually paid are a fixed percentage of the
recipient's income. However, each local housing authority establishes its own income
limits and rental rates so that a regional measure can pick up only part of the variation in
subsidy values. Consequently, benefits are constrained to be no less than zero.

ble. First, the distributional effects could simply be ignored—not because they are unimportant but because, as with direct government expenditures, the task is simply too large to do adequately. An exhaustive study of tax incidence is beyond the scope of this research. A second possible approach is to use another researcher's results on tax incidence to approximate these burdens. Following the sections on income and payroll taxes, this research examines the results from one recent study on the incidence of all taxes, but only to illustrate the distributional consequences of omitting the remaining taxes.

Income Tax

This research assumes that the income tax is not shifted by the taxpayer. Moreover, several simplifying assumptions facilitate the imputation of tax liabilities for each family. First is the assumption that all aged families file separately, even if they reside in larger extended family groups; second, that they take full advantage of tax exemptions available to them. In actuality, a lack of perfect knowledge about these benefits may preclude their use, so that this research may be understating taxes actually paid by aged families.

In general, this study employs the simplifying assumptions of Hall (1973, pp. 118–21) and Taussig (1973, pp. 18–19). Taxable income includes earned income, dividends, interest and rental income, private pensions, and the "other" income category. No attempt has been made to value capital gains. From taxable income a $600 personal exemption for each family member is deducted. In addition, the standard deduction is estimated as $200 plus $100 for each family member or 15 percent of taxable income, whichever is higher. Calculations by Taussig suggest that the 15 percent figure is a closer approximation of standard and itemized deductions for all income classes than the actual statutory provisions.[24]

These computations yield the estimated tax for young families. For aged families, tax liabilities also include an estimate of three tax expenditures. The definition of taxable income implicitly captures one of these tax expenditures—the exclusion of government transfer income. The remaining two added here are the retirement income tax credit and the extra $600 exemption allowed all persons over sixty-five. Total income tax liability for aged families (T_t^y) can thus be ex-

[24] Although for 1966 there was a legal $1,000 limit on the standard deduction, the 15 percent reduction evidently captures other provisions in the tax laws which limit the liability of persons at higher income levels.

pressed in dollars as:

$$T_t^y = k[y - d - 600(n + a)] - TC$$

where

   y = taxable income
   k = appropriate tax rate
   d = deduction which is maximum of $.15y$ or $[200 + 100(n)]$
   n = number of persons in the aged family
   a = number of persons sixty-five and over
   TC = retirement income tax credit.

The retirement income tax credit permits a reduction in tax liability of up to $228.60. This provision allows a credit against taxes of 15 percent of property income, private pensions, and other forms of nonearned income up to a maximum of $1,524.[25] The benefits of this provision mainly affect those whose primary source of income is property or taxable annuities.

Payroll Taxes

The incidence of the payroll tax for Social Security has become a controversial subject.[26] At issue is who bears the burden of the employer's contribution to this tax. In 1966, employees paid 4.2 percent of any wages up to $6,600. An equal amount constituted the employer's contribution. It is Brittain's (1971) contention that labor bears the burden not only of the tax it pays directly but also of the employer's share. He argues that the entire tax comes out of the real demand price of labor and that there are few employment effects. In disagreeing with Brittain's analysis, Feldstein (1972) asserts that the only conclusion which can be drawn is that labor would bear the burden "if the supply of labor and capital were not changed by the tax" (p. 375). The burden of at least the employer's portion of the tax would consequently be shifted onto consumers of labor-intensive goods.

The payroll tax estimate used here assumes that the employer

---

[25] This ceiling is doubled for a couple filing jointly when both are over sixty-five. Consequently, the maximum potential credit becomes $457.20. However, income from earnings and Social Security payments reduce the credit. Social Security results in a dollar for dollar reduction of the $1,524 allowable income. Earnings of up to $1,200 do not affect the credit. Beyond $1,200, the tax rate on earnings is 50 percent up to $1,700 and 100 percent beyond $1,700—again applied against nonearned income up to a limit of $1,524.

[26] See, for example, Brittain (1971, 1972) and Feldstein (1972).

bears the full burden of the tax—a total of 8.4 percent of earnings for workers and 6.15 percent for self-employed individuals. This is the more progressive of the two incidence assumptions. Since no consumption data are available in the SEO, this study cannot estimate the case where the tax is shifted onto consumers. However, calculations by Pechman and Okner (1974) indicate that in the latter case, the incidence of payroll taxes would place a greater burden on the aged in general, with lower-income aged families bearing a particularly large share of the tax burden.

Other Taxes

Recent work by Pechman and Okner (1974) using the SEO merged with IRS data represents one of the most thorough estimates of tax incidence to date. Using several different assumptions about shifting and incidence, the authors calculated the effects of six different taxes on the population by income class. They also made estimates for several subgroups of the population, including the aged.

Table 3.5 shows estimated liabilities by aged income class for the four taxes not estimated here, based on the most progressive assumptions. Pechman and Okner concluded that with the exception of the lowest income groups the effective tax rates do not vary greatly by income, regardless of the incidence assumptions used. As table 3.5 illustrates, the generalization also holds for the combined effect of the four tax categories for the aged using the progressive incidence assumptions. The taxes comprise about 15 percent of income, rising only slightly for the highest income class.[27]

While the Pechman–Okner estimates could be subtracted from the measure of economic welfare to complete the tax estimates for this study, little would be gained. The absolute level of economic welfare would fall, but as shown in table 3.5, inclusion of the taxes would have little effect on the equality of the distribution. Moreover, tax liabilities are available only by income class, suppressing many of the important differences in actual tax liabilities for aged families which would arise because of differences in consumption habits and wealth. Thus, the Pechman–Okner results are included here only to illustrate the incidence and relative size of other taxes for the aged.

[27] Actually, the Pechman–Okner results are more redistributive for the aged if personal income and payroll taxes are included. The effective tax rates in that case range from about 15 percent for the lower income classes to over 25 percent at the higher levels. By the least progressive estimates, taxes as a share of adjusted family income are higher for low income families. In this case, there is some redistribution toward higher income families.

TABLE 3.5
Estimates of Incidence of "Other" Taxes for Families Headed by Persons over Sixty-Five

Population Decile	Corporation Income Tax	Property Tax	Sales and Excise Tax	Personal Property and Motor Vehicle Taxes	Total "Other" Taxes	Effective Tax Rates*
Lowest 5 percent	$ 10	$ 14	$ 112	$ 4	$ 140	15.5%
Second 5 percent	61	70	268	8	407	13.7
Second decile	242	312	623	28	1205	14.6
Third decile	416	454	516	25	1411	17.1
Fourth decile	382	423	415	25	1225	17.2
Fifth decile	378	364	354	21	1117	17.2
Sixth decile	356	320	345	16	1037	15.7
Seventh decile	391	333	324	24	1072	16.5
Eighth decile	335	239	230	12	616	12.4
Ninth decile	673	546	506	20	1745	15.7
Tenth decile	5,675	3,306	1,149	56	10,186	22.4
Total	*8,929*	*6,371*	*4,851*	*239*	*20,390*	*18.8*

SOURCE: Table E–37, Appendix E, unpublished supplement to Pechman and Okner (1974).
* Taxes are expressed as percentages of adjusted family income.

INTRAFAMILY TRANSFERS

As was discussed in chapter 2, little has been done to estimate the effect of intrafamily transfers among family subgroups living together in extended units. The estimation procedure used here incorporates available information to derive a conservative value for such transfers. Intrafamily transfers can have either a positive or a negative effect on the economic welfare of an elderly family. Aged family members, may be the recipients of a subsidy or they may be providers of support (a negative subsidy to the aged family). The direction of the flow and the amount of aid is assumed to be a function of both the level of economic welfare for each family and the needs of each as determined by family size and composition. Two assumptions dictate the form of the equation. First, this approach assumes that the highest priority of the extended family is to ensure all its members a subsistence level of consumption. Second, for families with resources greater than subsistence, subsidies to the "needy" subfamily rise as the level of total extended family economic welfare rises, but less than proportionally. That is, an elderly person residing with relatives would benefit from the younger members' higher level of economic welfare but it is unlikely that the aged person would receive a proportional share of total family resources.

For extended families whose total welfare is less than or equal to a subsistence standard (poverty threshold), these assumptions dictate that the welfare ratios of each subfamily be equalized. Everyone in the extended family shares equally the burden of too few resources. When total family well-being is high enough to ensure each subfamily a welfare ratio greater than one, the "needy" subfamily is still subsidized (and assured a welfare ratio greater than or equal to one) but its welfare ratio remains less than that of the donor subfamily. The higher the total extended family's welfare ratio and the higher the welfare ratio of the recipient family, the greater is the resulting difference between the welfare ratios. To achieve this, the equation that equalizes the welfare ratios is multiplied by the function (δ). The "donor" family, assigned a subscript of 1, is always the subfamily with the higher welfare ratio. Thus, intrafamily transfers are calculated by the following formula:

$$I_{12} = \delta[p_2(W)/(p_1 + p_2) - W_2]$$

where

$$\delta = \begin{cases} 1 & \text{when} \quad W - p_1 - p_2 \leq 0 \\ (f_1 - f_2)/(f_1 + f_2) & \text{when} \quad W - p_1 - p_2 > 0 \end{cases}$$

I_{12} = intrafamily transfer from subfamily 1 to 2

W = total level of economic welfare for extended family

$i = \begin{cases} 1 \text{ if donor subfamily} \\ 2 \text{ if recipient subfamily} \end{cases}$

W_i = that portion of the welfare (in dollars) attributable to subfamily i

p_i = the poverty threshold for subfamily i

$f_i = W_i/p_i$, the welfare ratio.

When δ equals 1, the welfare ratios of each subfamily are equalized.[28] However, for extended families with resources above a subsistence level, δ is greater than zero but less than one since W_1/p_1 is by definition larger than W_2/p_2. Thus, when δ is multiplied by the welfare equalization formula, an increase in the donor family's level of economic welfare is only partially passed on to the recipient family. If, for some reason, the welfare ratio for the recipient family increases, its intrafamily subsidy falls but by less than the amount of the original increase. Again, the exact fraction depends upon the family's total welfare ratio.[29]

The measure of economic welfare (W) used in the above equations consists of the previously derived components with the exception of public housing. This housing subsidy is assumed to affect the entire extended family and has been estimated on that basis. The same computational methods yield the level of welfare for the younger subfamilies. (See Appendix B for a more detailed description.)

To test the sensitivity of the measure to the formula proposed here, two alternative allocation procedures are also estimated. First, a lower bound on intrafamily transfers assumes that donor subfamilies transfer only enough resources to ensure a subsistence level for their dependent members. Using the poverty threshold as a benchmark for

---

[28] It can be shown that when $I_{12} = 0$, $W_1/p_1 = W_2/p_2$. That is

$$p_2(W_1 + W_2)/(p_1 + p_2) = W_2$$
$$p_2(W_1 + W_2) = W_2(p_1 + p_2)$$
$$W_1 p_2 = W_2 p_1$$

[29] The first derivative of δ with respect to W_1 is between 0 and 1 and the second derivative is negative—indicating that as W_1 increases, δ increases at a decreasing rate. That is

$$\partial\delta/\partial W_1 = 2p_1 p_2 W_2/[(W_1 p_2)^2 + 2p_1 p_2 W_1 W_2 + (W_2 p_1)^2].$$

The opposite is true for W_2. The first derivative is between 0 and −1 and the second derivative is positive:

$$\partial\delta/\partial W_2 = 2p_1 p_2 W_2/(W_1 p_2 + W_2 p_1)^2.$$

such a level of living, recipient families would receive only an amount sufficient to bring them up to p_2. For families where all members already have resources that exceed their poverty threshold no transfers occur. On the other hand, this alternative equalizes the welfare ratios of each subfamily when total family welfare is below subsistence.

An estimate for the upper bound on intrafamily transfers is obtained by assuming that extended families always equalize the welfare ratios of the subfamilies. Regardless of the absolute level of economic status, all family members share equally in the available resources. This is comparable to using the formula as first presented, but always setting δ equal to one. Such a formulation certainly represents the most generous possible transfer.

Actually, all three estimates of intrafamily transfers remain the same when total family welfare is below a subsistence level. The discrepancies arise at higher levels of economic status and when the resources of the subfamilies differ substantially. If, for example, the recipient members are aged, their level of economic status may only be raised to their poverty threshold under the lower bound or they may share equally—in proportion to need—with the younger members (the upper bound). When the younger family members have substantial resources, the differences in estimated transfers can be large indeed. The original formula provides an intermediate estimate within these two bounds.

An important issue concerning the influence of intrafamily transfers on the welfare of the aged is the role of the extended family versus the role of government in providing support to needy aged persons. Essentially, the treatment here assumes that part of the incidence of any government tax or transfer directed at the aged will fall on the younger subfamily. That is, benefits to the aged from the expansion of a government program or the adoption of a new program will be partially shared by the younger members of the extended family. Moreover, this remains true whether the aged subfamily is a donor or a recipient in the above formulation.

When government transfers are examined in chapter 5 by "pulling them out" of the distribution, intrafamily transfers will be recomputed each time. Therefore, aged families who reside with relatives will not suffer the full loss of the transfer since it will be spread among the extended family group. Such treatment of extended families does presume to answer the question of why government seems to have taken over an area which was previously the responsibility of relatives, but it should yield a better measure of transfer incidence for aged persons residing with relatives.

4

The Distribution of Economic Welfare

Although the ultimate goal of this research is the evaluation of government programs based on a more comprehensive measure of economic welfare, the distribution of the well-being of aged families is itself of interest. This chapter examines the distribution of income of aged families and analyzes the contribution of each of the measured components of the economic status measure. The final indicator of economic status is derived by adding, in sequence, each of the components described in chapter 3. Comparisons are made between the final cumulative distribution of economic welfare and the distribution using current money income. In addition, this chapter disaggregates the demographic characteristics of the aged by income and economic welfare status.

PRESENTATION OF RESULTS

It is important first to note that order does matter in assessing the distributional consequences of a particular component. For example, the annuitized value of net worth would have a different effect on the distribution depending upon whether or not cash transfers were already included. The ordering begins with those components most closely allied with current income. Net worth is added next, then government transfers and taxes, and finally, intrafamily transfers. Intrafamily transfers come last since their calculation depends upon all the earlier components. Therefore, while a reasonable ordering for the inclusion of these components has been attempted, caution should be taken in the interpretation of marginal changes in the distribution.

The summary statistics in tables 4.1 and 4.4 facilitate comparisons across distributions. The median indicates the level of economic welfare attributable to the family at the fiftieth percentile, below which half of the aged families have lower levels of welfare or income. The mean of the distribution simply calculates the average dollar amount across all families. The "under $2,000" statistic is the percentage of families with levels of welfare under $2,000; this figure roughly corresponds to the Orshansky (1968, p. 5) value for poor aged couples in 1966.[1] While this percentage is valuable in illustrating the proportion of families under certain dollar amounts, it should not be interpreted for this research as indicating the percentage of families in poverty. The Social Security Administration (SSA) establishes poverty figures for application with current money income. When an expanded life-cycle measure is used, the SSA figures are no longer applicable. For example, the threshold budgets contain no provisions for health expenditures. Medicare estimates in the economic welfare measure provide at least $131 to each individual over sixty-five. Even if only one person of an aged couple were over sixty-five, such a benefit would account for almost 7 percent of the couple's poverty threshold. Thus, the percentage of families under the $2,000 level provides a benchmark for comparison, illustrating the proportion of families under an arbitrarily set standard, and does not indicate the number of poor.

Finally, the Gini coefficient in table 4.4 summarizes each intermediate distribution. This measure indicates the degree of inequality that exists within a distribution by estimating the area between the line of equality and the Lorenz curve. The smaller the Gini coefficient, g, the more equal is the distribution. Values range between zero and one, and are calculated by the following formula:

$$g = 1 - \sum_h \left(\frac{K_h - K_{h-1}}{K} \right) \left(\frac{CY_h + CY_{h-1}}{Y} \right)$$

where

K_h = number of family units with income below the hth income class limit

CY_h = cumulative total income of all the K_h family units

K = total family units

Y = total income of all K family units.

The Gini coefficient is insensitive to the extremes of the distribution. Moreover, as Atkinson (1970) has pointed out, unless the Lorenz

---

[1] The actual value is $1,970. See Orshansky (1968, p. 5).

curves never cross, the Gini coefficient implies a particular social welfare function. For the Gini, the function attaches more weight to transfers affecting middle income classes. Atkinson advocates making explicit the particular welfare function and hence the degree of "inequality aversion." For the present research, the Gini is included for comparison since it is the most commonly used summary statistic in distributional studies. Moreover, this chapter presents the actual distributions, reducing reliance on this statistic.

CURRENT MONEY INCOME

The measure of current money income is of interest for comparison with the intermediate and final distributions of economic welfare. The assumptions about family composition which are used to compute money income and the economic welfare distributions diverge from standard definitions; the resulting distributions can vary substantially when these definitions change. Consequently, this section briefly examines the effect of the assumptions on the distribution of current income.

The definition of family composition used in this research differs in two respects from the traditional approach. First, most studies count as aged only those families where the head is over sixty-five. An aged family in this research is any family containing at least one member sixty-five or over. In addition, where aged persons reside in extended families, income and the level of economic welfare are measured for each separate subfamily.[2] Such an approach permits a measure of the contribution of relatives within the household and facilitates comparisons with aged persons residing independently. Standard treatments use the income of the entire extended family unit (if headed by someone sixty-five or over).

Table 4.1 presents three distributions to illustrate the differences which result from this alternative definition. The first column displays income for families with any member sixty-five or over, and is restricted to the income of the aged nuclear family in an extended unit; this is the definition used in this research. In the second column income from extended families is not disaggregated by subfamily. Thus, the conversion of family income to equivalency units to standardize the distribution includes all income, and the poverty threshold measure includes the entire family unit. When this change is made, the

[2] Again, the subfamily consists of all aged persons and their spouses. All younger adults and children are treated as one young subfamily.

TABLE 4.1

Percentage Distributions of Aged Families by Alternative Definitions of Family Composition

Dollar Values	Distribution A*	Distribution B*	Distribution C*
Negative	.13%	.14%	.15%
$ 0	1.92	.52	.60
1–499	3.38	1.10	1.27
500–999	8.84	5.34	5.94
1000–1499	13.49	10.13	11.50
1500–1999	12.88	11.62	13.12
2000–2499	11.37	10.27	11.41
2500–2999	8.87	8.96	9.56
3000–3999	13.02	13.46	13.77
4000–4999	7.26	9.10	8.35
5000–5999	5.37	7.77	6.79
6000–7999	5.56	9.41	7.30
8000–9999	2.91	5.43	4.57
10,000–14,999	3.06	4.57	3.60
15,000+	1.93	2.18	2.07
Median income	$2396	$3143	$2835
Mean income	$3448.86	$4282.39	$3930.63
Under $2000	40.71%	28.85%	32.58%

* A = As used in this research, i.e., families with any member sixty-five or over and restricted to aged subfamily in extended family.
 B = Treating extended family as one unit.
 C = Treating extended family as one unit and limited to families headed by an aged person.

number of families below $2,000 falls from 41 percent in the first distribution (Distribution A) to 29 percent in the second (Distribution B). This dramatic difference indicates the potential contribution of other relatives to the aged members. Income which is attributable to aged members of a larger unit is evidently less in proportion to their needs than the income-to-needs ratio for the total extended family unit.

The third distribution (Distribution C) employs the same treatment of extended family income as the second. However, for this distribution only families headed by aged persons are included. The first two distributions contain families in which any member is sixty-five or over—including the spouse or other relative of the head. This definitional change is also revealing about the economic status of the aged. The proportion of families with incomes under $2,000 goes up by more than 3 percentage points, again underscoring the impact of living arrangements on the well-being of the aged. Designation of a younger member as head often corresponds to higher total family income, since the head is usually the principal earner. Because this third definition contains extended families only when they are headed by an elderly person, the distribution omits the "higher income" extended units. Thus, this latter commonly used definition understates aged family income.

THE COMPONENTS OF THE ECONOMIC WELFARE MEASURE

Although this chapter emphasizes the effect of certain components on the distribution of economic welfare and the subsequent ranking of aged families, it is also important to note the relative size of each component (see table 4.2). These figures do not, however, capture

TABLE 4.2
Components of Economic Welfare

Component	Average per Aged Family	Percentage of Families Receiving	Average per Recipient Family
Money income components*			
Earnings	$1209.87	32.77%	$3692.00
Permanent portion**	490.55	32.77	1496.95
"Other" income	46.09	4.81	958.21
Private pensions	156.50	11.50	1360.87
Cash transfers			
Social Security	1098.19	81.11	1353.95
Public assistance	80.63	10.29	783.58
Government pensions	216.24	10.59	2041.93
Veterans' benefits	86.47	9.41	918.92
Unemployment and workmen's compensation	9.75	2.80	348.21
Annuity	2950.52	81.48	3621.16
In-Kind transfers			
Medicare	247.17	100.00	247.17
Medicaid	115.45	33.58	343.81
Public housing	4.84	1.28	378.13
Taxes			
Income	150.67	19.23	783.52
Payroll	67.32	30.52	220.58
Intrafamily transfers			
Positive		15.64	1652.31
Negative	−1.03	12.66	−2049.43

* Excludes property income.
** This is the estimated portion of earnings that would be replaced from other sources upon retirement and corresponds to the amount included in the money income part of the measure.

exact population aggregates for 1966 for several reasons. The size of each component has been converted into "equivalent" dollars for an aged couple.[3] In addition, there are problems with the data. Cash transfers are generally presumed to be underreported in the SEO, and the computations for in-kind transfers are affected by missing data. Thus, these amounts are only indicative of the *relative* size of each component.

For those still in the labor force, earnings obviously constitute an important source of well-being. Nonetheless, overall average earnings are small relative to both cash transfers and the net worth annuity. However, some of the annuity is attributable to the transitory portion of earnings. This study classifies just over 40 percent of all wages and salaries as permanent income—income which would be replaced by various pension programs upon a worker's retirement. In addition to Social Security, public and private pensions provide substantial benefits, but to a limited number of aged families.

Those transfer programs often thought to be oriented exclusively to low income groups, such as public assistance, public housing, and Medicaid, are small in size by comparison with other government transfers. These three transfers comprise only about 11 percent of the total included here, largely because of the limited number of families affected by the transfers. The components which provide the most extensive coverage of aged families are Medicare, Social Security, and the annuity estimate. Intrafamily transfers alter the well-being of only 28 percent of aged families, and the average across all aged families is very small. However, the absolute value of these resource flows is substantial. The overall mean is low because the transfers are offsetting. When aged members are the donors, they provide larger transfers on average than when the aged are the recipients. However, slightly more families receive positive transfers. In general, then, it can be said that the nonmoney income components of economic welfare are very important to the aged.

Table 4.3 groups the components into five broad headings to display the range of benefits provided. The first group, money income, includes the "permanent" portion of earnings, other private income sources, and cash transfers. Most families have incomes under $5,000 from these sources. The annuity and intrafamily transfer components

[3] A more complete discussion of equivalency units was presented in chapter 3. Basically, the level of welfare for an unrelated individual is scaled up to a level comparable to an aged couple and is similarly scaled down for larger families. Consequently, it is not necessary to depict a different distribution for each family size and composition since the equivalency units adjust the welfare values for these characteristics.

TABLE 4.3
Distributions for Components of Economic Welfare Measure

Income Class	Money Income	Annuity	In-Kind Transfers	Taxes	Intrafamily Transfers
Less than −$5000	0 %	.10%	0 %	.39%	.83%
−4999−−2000	0	.18	0	2.11	2.46
−1999−−1000	0	.16	0	5.04	2.21
−999−−1	0	2.59	0	26.58	6.61
0	3.50	18.52	0	65.87	72.24
1−999	15.40	29.93	98.32	0	7.60
1000−1999	33.29	16.31	1.68	0	3.63
2000−4999	43.11	19.03	0	0	3.39
5000−9999	4.40	7.15	0	0	.85
10,000 or more	.30	5.87	0	0	.12
Mean	$2184.21	$2950.52	$381.34	$−217.76	$−1.03

both provide a wider range of values, while taxes and in-kind transfers are largely confined to subtracting or adding less than $2,000 to the level of economic status.

These generalizations are borne out when each component group is added sequentially to derive the final distribution of economic welfare in table 4.4. The first intermediate distribution consists of the money income portion. To that are added the remaining components in the same order as in table 4.3: the annuity estimate, in-kind transfers, taxes, and intrafamily transfers. The current money income distribution is more comprehensive than the first intermediate measure, since it excludes property income and part of earnings. Thus, the mean and median are higher for current money income while there are fewer families with less than $2,000. However, a comparison of the second intermediate distribution with current income dramatically reverses the situation. The number of families with total resources under $2,000 drops by 14 percentage points with the substitution of the annuity for interest income. The median dollar value rises by more than $1,000. In addition, the Gini coefficient increases substantially, indicating a less equal distribution.

The addition of in-kind transfers also has a sizable effect on the distribution, largely as a result of the assumption that all aged families receive Medicare benefits. Again the number of families below the $2,000 level drops substantially, and the mean rises by almost $400. The inclusion of tax liabilities has little effect on those families at the bottom of the distribution who escape income tax liability. However, the mean falls as families at higher levels incur these liabilities. Both

TABLE 4.4
Distributions for Current Income and the Intermediate and Final Measures of Economic Welfare

Dollar Values	Current Income	Intermediate 1	Intermediate 2	Intermediate 3	Intermediate 4	Final 5
Negative	.13%	0 %	.32%	.22%	.22%	.18%
$ 0	1.92	3.50	1.30	0	0	0
1–499	3.38	3.23	2.31	.99	.99	.22
500–999	8.84	12.18	6.25	3.08	3.08	1.55
1000–1499	13.49	17.13	7.64	6.01	6.01	4.38
1500–1999	12.88	16.14	9.06	7.77	8.03	8.02
2000–2499	11.37	13.77	7.57	9.15	9.35	9.23
2500–2999	8.87	11.33	8.10	8.56	9.16	9.76
3000–3999	13.02	14.09	13.02	16.35	17.23	18.96
4000–4999	7.26	3.93	11.24	11.60	11.96	13.07
5000–5999	5.37	2.52	7.60	8.73	8.99	9.91
6000–7999	5.56	1.55	9.65	10.89	9.74	10.32
8000–9999	2.91	.33	5.42	5.45	5.20	5.25
10,000–14,999	3.06	.20	5.64	6.18	5.28	4.77
15,000 or more	1.93	.09	4.88	5.02	4.74	4.38
Median	$2396	$1932	$3572	$3870	$3764	$3879
Mean	$3448.86	$2184.21	$5131.26	$5510.17	$5291.41	$5279.85
Under $2000	40.71%	52.18%	26.88%	18.07%	18.33%	14.35%
Gini Coefficient	.458	.469	.482	.443	.437	.403

NOTE: The intermediate and final measures include the following:

1. $Y_t^{e*} + O_t + G_t^c$
2. $Y_t^{e*} + O_t + G_t^c + S_t^*$
3. $Y_t^{e*} + O_t + G_t^c + S_t^* + G_t^{k*}$
4. $Y_t^{e*} + O_t + G_t^c + S_t^* + G_t^{k*} - T_t^*$
5. $Y_t^{e*} + O_t + G_t^c + S_t^* + G_t^{k*} - T_t^* + I_t$

of these components reduce the Gini coefficient, reflecting the equalizing influence of the taxes and in-kind transfers. Finally, intrafamily transfers reduce both tails of the distribution and raise the median slightly. This then causes a large drop in the Gini coefficient. About 4 percent fewer families have resources below $2,000 as a result of this transfer.

Current Income and the Measure of Economic Welfare

A large number of families rise above the $2,000 line when the final measure replaces money income. However, it is more significant that even with substantial opportunities to move up, over 14 percent of all aged families remain below the $2,000 line. Although the 1966 Orshansky poverty threshold measure of $1,970 for an aged couple applies only to current income, it is nonetheless important to note that the inclusion of these additional nonmoney resources still cannot raise all families over this benchmark.

Comparisons of the final distribution of economic welfare and money income are displayed graphically in figure 4.1. Overall, the economic welfare measure lies to the right of current income and the shape of the distribution also changes somewhat. The distribution of economic welfare is more equal than that of current income. The Gini coefficient for income is .458 but falls to .403 for the economic welfare measure. While including the annuity value for net worth creates more inequality, the other nonincome components—taxes, in-kind transfers, and intrafamily transfers—all increase the equality of the distribution.

Table 4.5 indicates differences in the ranking of families within the distribution depending upon whether current income or the economic welfare measure is used. Both distributions are divided into quintiles. Each row of the table indicates where families in each quintile of income rank when measured by economic welfare. Families do not benefit uniformly from the additional resources included in the economic welfare measure. For example, only about one-half (11.5 percent) of the bottom 20 percent of families by current income are also in the lowest quintile by the economic welfare measure. The off-diagonal figures indicate those families raised or lowered in rank by the economic welfare measure. Just over 30 percent of all aged families fall by quintile ranking when the measure of economic status is used. As compared to current income, 25.7 percent of elderly families show an increase by one or more quintiles when subjected to the expanded measure. A larger percentage of families move up by

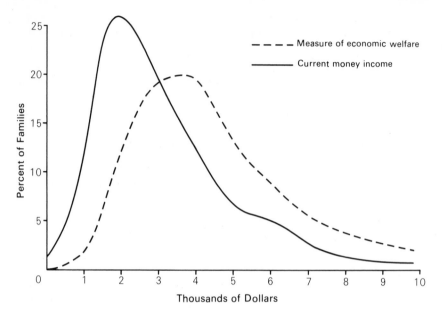

FIGURE 4.1 Relative frequency distributions of economic welfare and current money income.

more than one quintile than fall by two or more quintile classes. Thus, the measure of economic welfare derived here affects the absolute level of resources available to a family, the equality of the distribution, and the ranking of families within the distribution as compared with current money income.

As was indicated earlier, the most important nonincome compo-

TABLE 4.5
Comparison of Quintile Rankings of Aged Families by Current Income and Economic Welfare Measure

| Current Income | Economic Welfare Measure | | | | | |
	First Quintile	Second Quintile	Third Quintile	Fourth Quintile	Fifth Quintile	Total
First quintile	11.5%	3.5%	2.3%	1.7%	1.0%	20.0%
Second quintile	5.7	7.5	3.7	2.0	1.1	20.0
Third quintile	1.4	6.2	6.6	3.6	2.2	20.0
Fourth quintile	1.1	2.0	5.1	7.2	4.6	20.0
Fifth quintile	0.3	0.8	2.3	5.5	11.1	20.0
Total	20.0	20.0	20.0	20.0	20.0	100.0

TABLE 4.6
Comparison of Mean Annuity Amounts of Aged Families by Current Income and Economic Welfare Measure

| Current Income | Economic Welfare Measure | | | | | |
	First Quintile	Second Quintile	Third Quintile	Fourth Quintile	Fifth Quintile	Total
First quintile	$ 215.32	$ 568.93	$1235.59	$2121.46	$ 4166.37	$ 742.96
Second quintile	192.22	675.46	1443.47	3734.37	9052.85	1470.82
Third quintile	595.64	421.87	1119.49	3064.56	9147.44	2090.47
Fourth quintile	761.45	858.42	913.68	2179.44	8072.23	2994.81
Fifth quintile	2397.64	1536.08	2323.46	2809.84	11371.06	7466.76
Total	306.92	632.11	1273.76	2659.82	9875.30	2950.52

nents of the measure are the annuity and intrafamily transfer estimates. They are also responsible for much of the change in the quintile rankings of aged families when the economic welfare measure replaces current income. Table 4.6 gives mean annuity values for aged families by quintile rankings. Holding income constant at, say, the second quintile, the annuity values rise dramatically by the level of economic status. Higher annuity values are undoubtedly one of the principal determinants of whether an aged family's economic status changes. Families with higher property income (and hence wealth) relative to earnings fare better by the measure of economic welfare adopted here.

Similarly, table 4.7 presents mean intrafamily transfers by income and economic welfare rankings. For those families residing in larger

TABLE 4.7
Comparison of Mean Intrafamily Transfers of Aged Families by Current Income and Economic Welfare Measure

| Current Income | Economic Welfare Measure | | | | | |
	First Quintile	Second Quintile	Third Quintile	Fourth Quintile	Fifth Quintile	Total
First quintile	$ 116.96	$974.98	$1620.80	$2431.41	$4141.32	$823.96
Second quintile	− 160.04	− 2.28	436.03	168.69	82.99	58.13
Third quintile	− 881.69	− 2.21	77.95	107.49	−240.01	− 47.19
Fourth quintile	−1530.39	−436.28	− 58.59	−117.82	−138.16	−221.41
Fifth quintile	−2104.94	−327.68	−662.86	−321.21	−719.76	−613.31
Total	− 170.14	114.74	200.37	99.64	−245.53	− 1.03

extended groups, transfers may be either positive or negative—reflecting transfers *by* the aged—depending upon the welfare-to-needs ratio of each subfamily. Thus it is not surprising that aged families that are in the lowest quintile by current income but who rank in, let us say, the highest two quintiles by the economic welfare measure are the recipients of substantial (positive) intrafamily transfers. It is unlikely that such families with incomes under $1,240 (the income limit for the first quintile) would have other resources sufficient to raise substantially their level of economic status. Analogously, those whose level of economic status falls from their current income ranking are likely to transfer some of their resources on to other relatives.

Alternative Annuity and Intrafamily Transfer Measures

Annuity Measures. As discussed in chapter 3, several alternative estimates of the net worth annuity are possible. These involve the treatment of current earnings. The calculation of a constant yearly annuity added to current income implies that for those families with labor force participants, economic status would probably be overstated. If the annuity remains at the same level when the workers retire, there will be a sharp decrease in potential consumption. Consequently, this particular approach is treated as the upper bound of possible annuity estimates. Current earnings are fully included in the money income component and the annuity is based only on net worth (see table 4.8).

The other extreme estimate assumes that all workers retire after the current period. Thus, the proper calculation of the annuity would add this year's earnings over and above what would normally be replaced by various retirement programs to net worth to be annuitized. This transitory portion of income will only accrue this year and thus should be spread over the remaining lifetime of the family members.

TABLE 4.8
Mean Values for Alternative Net Worth Measures

	Money Income Base	Annuity	Intermediate Distribution 2*
Lower bound	$2184.21	$2486.33	$4670.54
Estimate actually used	2184.21	2947.05	5131.26
Upper bound	2901.23	2420.54	5321.77

* $Y_t^{e*} + O_t + G_t^c + S_t^*$

As is indicated in table 4.8, the current income component is thus reduced by over $700. The annuity is increased, but only by $66.

The value used in this research comes closer to the upper bound by assuming that labor force participants remain on the job between two and five years longer rather than immediately retiring. This more realistic, although necessarily arbitrary, specification of labor market behavior results in a larger annuity but with the same money component base as that of the lower bound. While the mean of this alternative distribution is only $200 less than the upper bound, the calculation used here potentially has a large effect on aged families with high current earnings. These families may be among those in the highest quintile by current income who fall in rank by the economic welfare measure. For example, the number of families above the $10,000 level in the second intermediate distribution is 16 percent lower than would be the case if the upper bound measure were used. For those families with no aged earners—nearly two-thirds of the total—and for those with only moderate earnings, the alternative measure used would make little difference. The percentage of families under the $2,000 level varies by less than one percentage point regardless of the measure used.

Intrafamily Transfer Measures. The calculation of upper- and lower-bound estimates helps measure the sensitivity of the intrafamily transfer measure. The lower-bound estimate assumed that transfers were made only to raise the recipient family to a subsistence standard. The restricted nature of this transfer is shown in table 4.9. Negative transfers are larger, in part because younger families' "equivalency" values for economic status are standardized for a family of four. Thus, transfers to those relatives could total up to $3,345.

The upper-bound estimate totally equalized the welfare ratios of donor and recipient families, also an extreme assumption. Nearly 3.2 percent of all aged families gave or received transfers of more than $5,000. The intermediate estimate yielded mean values almost midway between the upper and lower bounds. Large transfers are also possible under this measure but are less frequent than for the upperbound estimates.

The effect of these alternatives on the distribution of economic welfare is most pronounced at the upper end of the distribution. Since in all three cases the positive and negative transfers tend to cancel each other in the mean, that statistic is not helpful in examining the sensitivity of the distribution. However, a comparison of the median values indicates that at $3,074 the lower bound is much below the other two alternatives ($3,879 and $3,985 for the intermediate- and

TABLE 4.9
Alternative Estimates of Intrafamily Transfers

Dollar Values	Lower Bound	Intermediate Estimate*	Upper Bound
Less than $-5000	0 %	.83%	1.49%
-4999--2000	2.42	2.46	3.82
-1999--1000	1.93	2.21	2.95
- 999--1	2.71	6.66	4.35
0	83.90	72.24	71.75
1-999	6.15	7.60	3.49
1000-1999	2.80	3.63	3.78
2000-4999	.11	3.39	6.70
5000-9999	0	.85	1.50
10,000 or more	0	.12	.19
Means			
Positive transfers	$-1516.47	$-2049.43	$-2274.82
Negative transfers	784.95	1652.31	2590.75
Overall	- 35.63	- 1.03	60.23

* This is the estimate used to derive the economic welfare measure.

upper-bound estimates). The discrepancy in the measures is confined to families over the $1,500 level since the lower-bound estimate diverges from the others only when families are close to or above the subsistence level ($1,970). At the upper end of the distribution, the lower-bound estimate results in slightly more families over the $10,000 level, since this alternative also restricts negative transfers. Obviously, then, the distribution of economic welfare is fairly sensitive to the alternative used. However, it is the lower-bound estimate—which is perhaps the least plausible—that displays the most variance. The upper-bound and intermediate estimates yield economic welfare distributions which do not substantially vary.

DEMOGRAPHIC CHARACTERISTICS AND THE ECONOMIC WELFARE MEASURE

Table 4.10 presents average income and economic welfare values by various demographic characteristics. Column 4 of the table calculates a ratio of welfare level to income in order to illustrate the relative gains or losses by various demographic groups. Thus, families headed by someone over eighty more than double their status when the expanded measure is used. By contrast, families with heads between sixty-five and sixty-nine show only a slight increase in well-being. The

TABLE 4.10
Average Income and Economic Welfare Values by Demographic Characteristics

Characteristic	1 Percentage of Families in Each Category	2 Mean Income	3 Mean Value for Economic Status Measure	4 Ratio 3/2*
Age of head				
18–64	14.79%	$2456.99	$4458.97	1.815
65–69	28.21	4396.80	5164.88	1.175
70–74	25.22	3923.95	5452.14	1.389
75–79	18.36	2865.25	5523.49	1.928
80–99	13.42	2454.82	5770.77	2.351
Race of head				
White	91.67	3585.75	5491.19	1.531
Nonwhite	8.33	1944.10	2953.30	1.519
Sex of head				
Male	64.98	4020.28	5837.65	1.452
Female	35.02	2376.65	4245.00	1.786
Family type				
Only aged members	65.25	3847.25	5920.03	1.539
Dependent children	6.47	2745.85	4345.98	1.583
Extended family	28.27	2690.35	4017.35	1.493
Work status of aged members				
Retired	68.85	2434.35	5059.64	2.078
Working	31.15	5696.23	5767.00	1.012
Residence				
Central city	32.66	3553.30	5035.71	1.417
Urban fringe	24.85	3880.53	6011.03	1.549
Not SMSA**	42.49	3106.17	5039.89	1.623
Region				
Northeast	25.54	3578.29	5116.86	1.430
North Central	32.02	3529.16	5408.41	1.532
South	29.04	2941.20	4650.43	1.581
West	13.40	4079.09	6647.46	1.630
Total	100.00	3448.86	5279.85	1.531

* Ratio of welfare level to income.
** SMSA = Standard Metropolitan Statistical Area as defined by U.S. Office of Management and Budget.

first age category captures mostly extended families where a younger member is designated as head. The aged members in this category receive positive intrafamily transfers which boost their economic status. For families over sixty-five, the increases in the ratio reflect the larger yearly annuity values which result from the lower life expectancy of older persons.

Both white and female heads of families also show larger increases in their economic status via the expanded measure. A more notable difference, however, occurs between families distinguished by the presence of aged labor force participants in the household. While those families whose aged members are all retired show a 200 percent increase on average, families with working members actually have only slightly higher average dollar amounts when the economic welfare measure is calculated.

The remaining three categories show little variation. Although living arrangements (i.e., "family type") may, as discussed above, greatly affect economic status, the average does not capture this. Residence and region are relatively neutral as might be expected, with nonurban residents and those in the West exhibiting the largest gains. The first five categories in this table are discussed below in more detail.

Average Age

Table 4.11 gives a quintile breakdown for average age. The low mean age for family head in the first income quintile reflects the number of income-poor elderly families residing in larger extended units. As discussed above, those families whose rankings by economic welfare increase from the first quintile of income often do so because

TABLE 4.11

Comparison of Average Age by Current Income and Economic Welfare Measure

	Economic Welfare Measure					
Current Income	First Quintile	Second Quintile	Third Quintile	Fourth Quintile	Fifth Quintile	Total
First quintile	69.2 yrs.	59.9 yrs.	60.4 yrs.	64.4 yrs.	65.0 yrs.	65.9 yrs.
Second quintile	70.7	72.1	69.0	73.4	77.3	71.6
Third quintile	71.1	71.0	71.6	72.5	75.0	71.9
Fourth quintile	69.9	67.7	69.6	71.2	74.4	71.1
Fifth quintile	64.8	65.4	65.2	67.8	70.7	69.0
Total	69.7	68.8	68.6	70.1	72.1	69.9

TABLE 4.12
Percentage of Families Headed by Nonwhites by Current Income and
Economic Welfare Measure

	Economic Welfare Measure					
Current Income	First Quintile	Second Quintile	Third Quintile	Fourth Quintile	Fifth Quintile	Total
First quintile	23.1%	10.0%	8.2%	6.4%	1.1%	16.7%
Second quintile	19.2	11.2	4.7	3.2	5.2	11.1
Third quintile	15.5	10.0	6.0	2.7	2.2	6.9
Fourth quintile	7.7	10.1	4.8	2.7	2.4	4.1
Fifth quintile	13.1	6.5	7.4	2.7	1.5	2.9
Total	20.4	10.3	5.8	3.0	2.0	8.3

of intrafamily transfers received. In such cases, the younger family members are likely to be designated as family head. A second notable figure is the high average age of household head for families in the uppermost quintile by the expanded measure. Since the annuity allocation is based on life expectancy, older aged families' annuity allocations would, ceteris paribus, tend to be larger.

Race

The high concentration of nonwhites in both the low income and low economic welfare quintiles underscores the lower levels of resources available to this group (table 4.12). Moreover, a proportionately larger number of families with nonwhite heads fall from higher quintile rankings by income to the first quintile by economic welfare. The incidence of poverty among minority races is high for any age group. Thus, the low levels of both current income and economic welfare undoubtedly reflect the higher poverty incidence among these families across their lifetimes. With a lower probability for high wage income or accumulated net worth, it is not surprising that these families are concentrated in the lower quintiles.

Living Arrangements

Over half of all aged families in the lowest quintile by income reside in extended family units, undoubtedly reflecting the dependence of these aged families on help from relatives (table 4.13). The percentages are even larger for families in that income class above the first quintile ranking by economic welfare. Similarly, many of the

TABLE 4.13
Percentage of Aged Families Living in Extended Units by Current Income and
Economic Welfare Measure

Current Income	Economic Welfare Measure					
	First Quintile	Second Quintile	Third Quintile	Fourth Quintile	Fifth Quintile	Total
First quintile	38.6%	70.5%	75.9%	75.0%	65.0%	52.6%
Second quintile	28.1	20.5	33.7	30.2	19.5	26.0
Third quintile	52.2	13.1	20.7	22.6	15.3	20.5
Fourth quintile	68.5	31.5	18.8	18.3	14.6	21.8
Fifth quintile	79.4	36.9	33.8	65.8	12.2	20.8
Total	39.1	28.8	30.2	27.1	16.1	28.3

donors of extended family transfers are likely to be found in the lowest quintile of economic welfare but are in the two highest quintiles of income (also see table 4.7). The smallest proportion of extended families is found in the highest quintile class of both income and welfare. These families are not dependent on relatives, and because few of them aid younger relatives, they remain in the top 20 percent regardless of the indicator used.

Labor Force Participation

When income is the indicator of economic status, families with labor force participants are more likely to fall into a higher quintile.

TABLE 4.14
Percentage of Families with at Least One Aged Labor Force Participant by Current
Income and Economic Welfare Measure

Current Income	Economic Welfare Measure					
	First Quintile	Second Quintile	Third Quintile	Fourth Quintile	Fifth Quintile	Total
First quintile	9.0%	8.7%	4.7%	6.7%	10.7%	8.4%
Second quintile	15.9	16.7	13.2	6.3	14.6	14.7
Third quintile	45.0	21.6	25.6	20.0	13.9	23.6
Fourth quintile	64.4	69.3	44.3	38.3	25.2	41.4
Fifth quintile	99.2	91.2	90.4	81.6	53.7	67.8
Total	18.4	24.9	32.9	41.3	38.4	31.1

Over two-thirds of families in the top 20 percent of income have at least one labor force participant (table 4.14). However, this relationship is much less pronounced for the economic welfare measure. Only 38 percent of families in the highest quintile by this measure have a wage or salary earner, an amount not substantially larger than the average across all families. Moreover, a larger percentage of those families who fall in rank when moving from income to the economic welfare measure have labor force participants. These figures illustrate the fact that persons with earnings (1) have those earnings adjusted downward by the annuity calculation, (2) are subject to higher taxes, and (3) are less likely to be eligible for Medicaid or public housing. Thus, the striking percentage differences in table 4.14 are to be expected.

Sex of Family Head

Table 4.15 displays the distribution of male heads of families by income and economic welfare class. As is usually assumed, many of the female-headed families are concentrated in the lowest 40 percent as ranked by income. However, for the economic welfare measure female-headed families tend to gain. There are fewer such families in the lowest quintile and more in the highest 20 percent of families ranked by the expanded measure. These female-headed families are less likely to have a labor force participant and more likely to reside in an extended household. Both of these factors lead to an increase (or at least no deterioration) in rank by the measure of economic status.

TABLE 4.15
Percentage of Families Headed by Male by Current Income and Economic Welfare Measure

	Economic Welfare Measure					
Current Income	First Quintile	Second Quintile	Third Quintile	Fourth Quintile	Fifth Quintile	Total
First quintile	38.1%	60.4%	64.7%	60.4%	64.7%	48.1%
Second quintile	46.0	51.4	55.3	48.2	45.3	49.9
Third quintile	57.5	62.0	71.8	58.4	55.4	63.6
Fourth quintile	64.5	69.5	83.1	85.0	77.2	80.0
Fifth quintile	74.3	81.9	82.9	82.7	83.9	83.2
Total	43.9	59.2	72.0	74.0	76.1	65.0

TABLE 4.16
Demographic Characteristics of the Aged Poor

Characteristic	Poverty Definition		
	Families Under $1,970		Relative Measure for Economic Welfare*
	Income	Economic Welfare	
Nonwhite family head	13.9%	22.7%	15.4%
Male family head	49.0	42.5	51.5
Extended family	39.3	47.5	34.0
With labor force participant	11.5	17.5	21.7
Average age	68.7 yrs.	69.5 yrs.	69.3 yrs.

* Since less than 15 percent of families are under $1,970 by the economic welfare measure versus 40 percent by current income, the relative measure consisting of the bottom 40 percent for economic welfare is also presented.

The Demographic Characteristics of the Poor

Forty percent of all aged families fall below the Social Security poverty threshold by a money income distribution. Thus, averaging across the bottom two quintiles of income gives the demographic characteristics for the income poor (table 4.16). In the case of the economic welfare distribution, less than 15 percent of families fall below the $1,970 threshold. The characteristics for this group are summarized in the second column. For further comparison, table 4.16 also summarizes the demographic characteristics for the bottom 40 percent by economic welfare. If poverty were considered a relative concept, this 40 percent figure would provide more appropriate figures for comparison.[4]

For both economic welfare specifications of the poor, families are, on the average, older and more likely to be headed by a nonwhite than they are when current income is used. The percentage of nonwhite family heads is particularly large by the absolute dollar measure for economic status. These are the families who remain at a very low level even after accounting for other potential sources of well-being. Also striking are the differences in the percentage of families with a labor

[4] Moreover, as has been discussed above, the money-income threshold should not be considered directly applicable when an expanded measure of economic status is used. The use of two separate figures thus reflects uncertainty about the exact definition of poverty by this measure. More research is needed towards this end.

force participant. In this case, the percentage rises most for the 40 percent economic welfare measure. The earnings adjustment causes more families with workers to fall into the lower two quintiles of the economic welfare measure, but a smaller percentage drop below $1,970 of measured resources.

For the remaining two characteristics, sex of family head and residence in extended families, the economic welfare figures diverge in opposite directions from the current income numbers. Male heads of families comprise a slightly larger proportion of the bottom two quintiles of economic status but drop sharply when the absolute dollar measure is used. While some female-headed families move up in rank by the expanded economic status measure, it appears that those at the very bottom (lowest 15 percent) do not. The same type of generalization can be made for aged families residing in extended units. A certain percentage with very low levels of resources may reside with younger relatives who are similarly disadvantaged. Thus, for the very poorest, residing in extended family units may not provide sufficient benefits to improve their economic status over current income. Indeed, some of these families may even transfer part of their own resources to younger relatives who also have very low resource levels.

Thus, there are substantive differences between the families at the bottom of the expanded measure and those in the lowest ranking by current income. Table 4.5 indicates that almost 30 percent of the families in the lowest two quintiles of income moved into the higher three quintiles of the economic status measure. Moreover, those moving up were not randomly drawn from the population. More families with younger heads and no labor force participants escaped the bottom two quintiles. Female-headed and white families also showed a greater proportional move out of the lowest 40 percent. Consequently, the expanded measure's rankings may yield different results when transfer and tax expenditure programs are examined in chapter 5.

5

The Impact of Government Programs on the Aged

Aged families and individuals receive a higher proportion of government tax expenditure and transfer programs than any other group in the United States. Moreover, government cash and in-kind transfer programs constitute 35 percent of the total measured economic welfare of the aged. This chapter examines the distributional effects of each of eleven major tax expenditure and transfer programs on both current money income and the measure of economic welfare. The analysis particularly emphasizes the impact of government programs on families at the bottom of each distribution. Earlier research in this area by Bridges (1967, 1970) suggested the general approach for this chapter.

PRESENTATION OF RESULTS

A comprehensive accounting of the contribution of each government program to the distribution of income or economic welfare would require more than a measure of the dollar benefits from the program. That is, the total differential should be computed, accounting for additional indirect changes in an aged family's income or welfare. Measuring the size of transfer or tax expenditure benefits yields only a partial derivative, implicitly assuming that all other variables remain constant. This latter procedure, which is used for this chapter, captures the ex post effect of a government program, assuming that the counterfactual is the existing distribution "minus" the dollar benefits to each family.[1]

This chapter computes the percentage of families for each class receiving benefits and the mean benefit per recipient in that class. These calculations use the distribution of welfare minus the particular program being examined to address the question of who among the aged benefit from government transfers and tax expenditures. A similar procedure is also employed to examine the effect of each cash transfer on current income. However, since current money income does not contain tax expenditures and in-kind transfers, no subtractions from this distribution are necessary to compute the effects of these programs.

Comparisons between current income and the economic welfare calculations illustrate how the distributional effects differ depending upon the measure used. Since for nearly every family dollars of welfare are higher than dollars of income, this analysis makes comparisons by taking a fixed percentage of families at the bottom of each distribution. For example, 41 percent of all aged families have less than $2,000 in current money income. For the economic welfare measure only 14.4 percent fall below this dollar amount. Consequently, the appropriate comparison is between benefits to the bottom X percent of families in both distributions rather than a comparison of benefits to those families below the same dollar amount in each distribution.[2]

Several measures of "target efficiency" serve as summary statistics for evaluating the effectiveness of each program in aiding families at the lower tail of the distribution. Target efficiency as defined by Weisbrod refers to the "degree to which the actual redistribution coincides with the desired redistribution" (1970, p. 125). Once the target group for a particular program has been identified, the proportion of total expenditures redistributed to that group can be calculated. This statistic displays the percentage of total expenditures received by the target group. Although many of the programs examined here have goals other

[1] Actually, the process used here is somewhat more complicated. Since intrafamily transfers are assumed to vary by the relative size of each subfamily's resources, these private transfers are recomputed for each new distribution when a transfer or tax expenditure is subtracted. When the aged family benefits more from a program than the younger members of an extended family, some of the benefits from the program are shifted to those younger members.

[2] Moreover, it is *not* correct to state that poverty among the aged has been reduced by the number of families moved over the $1,970 threshold. As mentioned previously, the Orshansky measures were designed for use with current money income and cannot be used to measure families in poverty when a broader definition of economic welfare is used.

than the distribution of resources to the aged poor, it is nonetheless of interest to examine a program's effectiveness in aiding this particular subgroup.

In a recent paper, Garfinkel and Kesselman (1976) criticized use of the target efficiency measure for comparing transfer programs. The major disadvantage of this measure arises from its inability to capture the net costs of the program to nonbeneficiaries. That is, the target efficiency measure may vary between two programs which actually provide equal benefits and costs net of taxes. This is an issue for comparing income-tested and non-income-tested programs in particular. The problem is exacerbated since the sources of revenue for the transfers and tax expenditures differ. The federal payroll tax provides funds for Social Security and Medicare. Unemployment and workmen's compensation programs are financed by special payroll taxes. Support for the remaining transfer and tax expenditure programs comes from the general fund. Thus, comparisons of Medicare and Medicaid, for example, must recognize the differences in sources of funding.

However, even with these strictures on its use, the target efficiency measure can provide useful information. When the transfers derive funding from the same source, or if they are competing for the same available funds, then some comparisons are legitimate. Certainly non-income-tested programs such as government pensions and Social Security should never be judged solely on their target efficiency to those at the bottom of the distribution of economic status. However, when they are suggested as effective poverty programs, an examination of their target efficiency rankings would be appropriate. In addition, comparisons of Social Security and Medicare or of public assistance and Medicaid can illuminate differences between cash and in-kind programs. Finally, the most important comparison—the differences in each program's target efficiency according to the measure used—avoids these problems.

Target efficiency measures for each tax expenditure and transfer are computed for both current income and the measure of economic welfare. Three target groups capture the lowest 15, 30, and 40 percent of families as measured by each distribution. Using percentages of families as the target group allows comparisons between distributions and among the various programs. Moreover, the three different percentages cover a range of families at the lower end of the distribution, offering a broader view of the impact of each program than would be possible if only one percentage were used. Finally, an additional summary measure combines target efficiency and the absolute size of each transfer.

Following a discussion of the ranking of government programs by these target efficiency standards, this chapter examines each transfer and tax expenditure individually. For each, a table detailing average benefits by income and welfare quintiles illustrates more fully the distribution of benefits and any discrepancies between the two measures. In addition, Appendix D contains tables for each program. These display the percentage of recipients and their average benefits by income and welfare class.[3]

AN OVERVIEW OF THE RESULTS

This section summarizes the effects of eleven major tax expenditure and transfer programs on both current money income and the measure of economic welfare. The specific cash transfers included are: Social Security and Railroad Retirement, government employee and military retirement programs, veterans' disability pensions and compensation, and public assistance. In-kind transfers include Medicare, Medicaid, and public housing. Finally, benefits from tax expenditures which are targeted directly at the aged—the double personal exemption, exclusion of Social Security and other transfer income, and the retirement income tax credit—are also examined.

Any comparison of these programs must be made with caution. The transfers and tax expenditures vary widely by size and distributional goals. As a consequence, while comparisons among the programs are of interest, no one statistic can offer conclusive evidence of their ultimate value to the aged. For example, one transfer might be very target efficient but, because of its size, benefit only a small number of people. Moreover, since there may be multiple goals for any one program, it is difficult indeed to rank the transfers in any meaningful way. This section compares these programs only as to their effectiveness in providing benefits to those at the bottom of each distribution.

The most striking result, seen in a comparison of table 5.1 with table 5.2, is the similarity in both the rankings of the transfers and the actual target efficiency measures. These findings might imply that the ranking of recipient families did not change beween the two distributions. Such an explanation seems to be valid for public assistance, for example, where benefits are both income and asset conditioned. How-

---

[3] Recipient benefits refer to averages for those who actually receive the transfer or tax expenditure. Averages per aged family are spread across both recipients and non-recipients.

TABLE 5.1
Target Efficiency Measures by Distribution of Current Income

Government Program	Percent of Benefits from Each Program to Aged Families in Lowest					
	15 Percent of Distribution	(Rank)	30 Percent of Distribution	(Rank)	40 Percent of Distribution	(Rank)
Cash transfers						
Social Security	14.40%	6	30.64%	6	41.32%	6
Public assistance	69.85	1	91.62	1	94.35	1
Government pensions	25.71	5	40.52	5	48.84	5
Veterans' benefits	27.03	4	42.98	4	53.53	4
Unemployment and workmen's comp.	10.79	8	23.37	8	27.57	8
In-kind transfers						
Medicare	13.06	7	26.35	7	35.82	7
Medicaid	28.83	3	56.00	3	73.83	3
Public housing	32.87	2	63.10	2	77.17	2
Tax expenditures						
Double exemption	trace	9	.13	9	.30	9
Exclusion of transfers	0	10	.02	10	.11	10
Retirement tax credit	0	10	.00	11	0	11

ever, table 4.5 has shown that a substantial number of families do shift by quintile ranking between the two distributions, making this explanation less likely for programs such as Medicare, unemployment compensation, and government pensions. Another plausible explanation is that for those families in the middle range of the income distribution whose rankings do change, benefits may be randomly distributed. These issues are discussed in more detail below. One notable exception to the similarities in target efficiencies is the much higher 15 percent figure for public housing when the economic welfare measure is used. It is also interesting that while all the target efficiencies of the three tax expenditures are very low, they are consistently better for the economic welfare distribution. Finally, unemployment compensation fares worse by the expanded definition of economic status.

Within each table, the rankings of the transfers based on target efficiency remain remarkably stable for all target groups. As would be expected, public assistance and public housing are quite target efficient. Although the Medicaid program is ranked third most efficient, its percentage falls substantially below the figures for public assis-

TABLE 5.2
Target Efficiency Measures by Distribution of Economic Welfare

Government Program	Percent of Benefits from Each Program to Aged Families in Lowest					
	15 Percent of Distribution	(Rank)	30 Percent of Distribution	(Rank)	40 Percent of Distribution	(Rank)
Cash transfers						
Social Security	16.08%	6	30.87%	6	40.65%	6
Public assistance	64.44	1	84.15	1	89.18	2
Government pensions	19.66	5	33.70	5	42.10	5
Veterans' benefits	27.55	4	42.98	4	53.28	4
Unemployment and workmen's comp.	3.91	10	17.26	8	28.16	8
In-kind transfers						
Medicare	12.63	7	26.09	7	35.53	7
Medicaid	29.44	3	57.91	3	71.42	3
Public housing	57.35	2	83.02	2	91.89	1
Tax expenditures						
Double exemption	5.93	8	12.14	9	17.96	9
Exclusion of transfers	2.34	11	5.20	11	10.10	10
Retirement tax credit	4.23	9	7.09	10	9.03	11

tance. Moreover, benefits are less than proportional for the Medicare program in every instance, and Social Security comes very close to being distributionally "neutral." While neither of these two programs is aimed specifically at low-income aged families, it is nonetheless important to note that they do not in any way favor the poor. The combined effect of unemployment insurance and workmen's compensation is particularly target inefficient. Finally, although the tax expenditure programs could a priori be expected to provide few benefits to aged families at the bottom of both distributions, in no case do they target substantial benefits to even the lower *half* of either distribution.

An alternative ranking of these programs presented in table 5.3 incorporates both size and target efficiency. Two rankings for each distribution are obtained by rating programs—from highest to lowest—by the *dollar* benefits they provide to the bottom 15 and 40 percent of families. Thus Social Security, which is by far the largest program (see table 4.2), always ranks first even though its target efficiency is lower. The interaction of target efficiency with size of program also changes other rankings. Government pensions and Medicare

TABLE 5.3
Transfer and Tax Expenditure Programs Ranked by Dollar Benefits Received

| | Ranking by Dollar Benefits Received by | | | |
| | Current Income | | Economic Welfare | |
Government Program	Lowest 15 Percent	Lowest 40 Percent	Lowest 15 Percent	Lowest 40 Percent
Cash transfers				
Social Security	1	1	1	1
Public assistance	2	5	2	5
Government pensions	3	2	3	4
Veterans' benefits	6	6	6	6
Unemployment and workmen's comp.	8	8	11	10
In-kind transfers				
Medicare	5	4	5	3
Medicaid	4	3	4	2
Public housing	7	7	7	9
Tax expenditures				
Double exemption	9	9	8	8
Exclusion of transfers	10	10	9	7
Retirement tax credit	10	11	10	11

both appear more favorable, while public housing, veterans' benefits, and public assistance fall in rank by absolute amounts of benefits. These last programs are target efficient but relatively small. The tax expenditures, which are both inefficient and restricted in size, remain at the bottom of both income rankings and fare only a little better via the economic welfare measure.

CASH TRANSFERS

The five categories of cash transfer programs examined here vary widely by size and distributional goals. Consequently, in addition to the rankings of the previous section, the benefits of each cash transfer are disaggregated by income and welfare class. The tables presented here provide further illumination of the distributional impact of each transfer and help explain discrepancies between the two economic status measures.

Social Security

The Social Security program comprises the largest single transfer to aged families. Combined with Railroad Retirement, it provided

TABLE 5.4

Mean Social Security Benefits by Current Income and Economic Welfare Measure

Current Income	Economic Welfare Measure					
	First Quintile	Second Quintile	Third Quintile	Fourth Quintile	Fifth Quintile	Total
First quintile	$1278.38	$1069.13	$ 975.76	$1000.98	$ 844.71	$1119.64
Second quintile	1044.99	1161.26	1107.95	1140.16	1386.36	1127.26
Third quintile	1106.78	1028.05	1328.46	1347.53	1380.47	1193.13
Fourth quintile	1123.56	1008.54	1073.52	1358.06	1412.69	1234.58
Fifth quintile	545.18	658.52	542.54	689.35	944.01	806.01
Total	1156.95	1061.88	1068.64	1085.90	1119.26	1098.19

benefits averaging $1,098.19 to 81 percent of all aged families in 1966. Social Security seeks both to replace earnings lost upon retirement and to boost the level of welfare of the aged poor.[4] Consequently, both the overall distribution of benefits and measures of target efficiency to the poor are of interest. In table D.1 (p. 125), recipient benefits remain reasonably constant across all income levels. The percentage of families receiving benefits also remains constant below $4,000. Above this income the percentage begins to decrease, accounting for the lower overall average in the highest income quintile (table 5.4). Since many of the families in the top fifth of income have members still in the labor force, the percentage receiving Social Security could thus be expected to be lower for this group.

There is no such drop for the highest quintile by the expanded measure, partly because earnings are adjusted downward. Thus, families with labor force participants are more evenly distributed across all quintile levels. The slightly higher target-efficiency measure for economic welfare results from the discrepancy in average benefits in the lowest quintile. Table D.1 (p. 125) indicates a somewhat higher percentage of families receiving Social Security in the lowest economic status brackets.

While the effects of subtracting Social Security from either distribution are not directly shown here, they are quite dramatic. For example, the number of families below the $2,000 level increases by 26 percentage points (to 67.8) when Social Security is excluded from current income. This change is attributable to the large size of the program rather than the proportion of total benefits targeted at this group.

[4] See Pechman, Aaron, and Taussig (1968, p. 55).

TABLE 5.5

Mean Public Assistance Benefits by Current Income and Economic Welfare Measure

| | Economic Welfare Measure | | | | | |
Current Income	First Quintile	Second Quintile	Third Quintile	Fourth Quintile	Fifth Quintile	Total
First quintile	$469.31	$196.84	$69.87	$19.40	$14.00	$336.12
Second quintile	61.94	63.94	5.50	44.16	3.45	45.73
Third quintile	31.11	11.79	10.82	9.03	.45	11.04
Fourth quintile	11.43	15.31	7.54	1.90	0	4.47
Fifth quintile	0	0	1.08	12.68	4.08	5.93
Total	309.80	64.33	13.07	11.71	3.10	80.63

Public Assistance

Public assistance programs for the aged are more modest in size than Social Security and are targeted solely at the low-income population. Consequently, both recipient benefits and the proportion of families receiving aid drop off quickly at higher income levels (table D.2, p. 126). The percentage of families with public assistance benefits also decreases dramatically by dollar class for the economic welfare measure. This is to be expected since states have stringent eligibility requirements for public assistance, which often include asset limits and account for any benefits from residing with relatives. Only 10.3 percent of all aged families received public assistance while more than 40 percent—by the definitions used here—fell below the Orshansky poverty threshold of $1,970 for an aged couple. Recipient benefits averaged $783.58—an amount sufficient to reduce the number of those under the money-income poverty threshold by just one percentage point.[5]

The stringency of the program helps to explain why this transfer excludes even families in the lowest income brackets. No more than 63 percent of families in any income class receive public assistance benefits. Table 5.5 illustrates that families ranked in the bottom 20 percent of both distributions receive by far the highest mean benefits. Increases in either the level of income or of economic welfare (reflecting the existence of assets or intrafamily transfers) result in a dramatic reduction in mean benefits. However, since higher levels of economic status can also be caused by receipt of in-kind transfers complementary to public assistance, the reduction in mean benefits is less pro-

[5] This estimate was obtained by calculating the distribution of income net of public assistance and the resulting percent of families below $1,970.

nounced by this measure than when income goes up. Recipient benefits in the lower income and welfare classes are higher than the $783.58 overall mean. Thus, the $459 figure in table 5.5 for the 20 percent of families at the bottom of both distributions indicates that, even for this group, public assistance coverage is not nearly universal. Only 53.3 percent of elderly families in this group receive benefits.

Government Pensions

As the second largest cash transfer to the aged, government pensions provide benefits to over 10 percent of elderly families. These benefits are based on previous government employment and are not income-conditioned. While the proportion of beneficiaries is about the same as it is for public assistance, pensions to recipients are higher, averaging $2,042. Table D.3 (p. 127) shows mean recipient pensions and the percentage of recipients in each income and welfare class. Except for some concentration in the lowest welfare and income classes, the proportions of recipients display no consistent pattern. The size of the pensions also seems to vary across the distributions in a random fashion.

Consequently table 5.6 also lacks, with one exception, a clearly discernible trend by which to compare the two distributions. Average benefits are highest in the bottom and top quintiles for both distributions. The lowest 20 percent of families by current income have larger mean benefits, explaining the discrepancy in the target efficiency measures. This reflects the importance of government pensions as an income component to recipients. For some families this may be the

TABLE 5.6

Mean Government Pension Benefits by Current Income and
Economic Welfare Measure

| | Economic Welfare Measure | | | | | |
Current Income	First Quintile	Second Quintile	Third Quintile	Fourth Quintile	Fifth Quintile	Total
First quintile	$318.18	$458.49	$289.37	$536.17	$522.72	$374.88
Second quintile	123.43	155.36	133.47	183.02	49.47	139.11
Third quintile	198.64	87.85	212.68	187.09	270.18	169.70
Fourth quintile	27.08	156.89	132.91	206.95	289.18	190.55
Fifth quintile	691.11	125.05	47.30	159.96	262.41	207.88
Total	242.79	188.79	164.35	219.64	271.65	216.24

main source of current income. Subtracting government pensions from income then causes some concentration of these families in the lowest quintile. Economic welfare, on the other hand, adds additional components, so that government pensions become relatively less important and recipient families are more evenly scattered across the distribution. Except for this difference, recipients and their benefit levels seem to be rather randomly distributed. Those who move up and down when the expanded measure is used would seem to "offset" each other, yielding reasonably similar target efficiency rankings.

Veterans' Benefits

Total benefits from veterans' pensions and compensation, averaging $86.47 per aged family, are slightly greater than public assistance benefits. Recipient families comprise 9.41 percent of the total aged population and receive a mean benefit of $918.92. When benefits by dollar class are compared between current money income and economic welfare, the proportion of recipients and average recipient benefits in each class tend to drop off more rapidly for current income (table D.4, p. 128). These effects are to be expected since at least part of veterans' benefits, the pensions, are income-conditioned.

Indeed, when mean benefits are shown by quintile rankings for the two distributions, the largest mean benefit accrues to families in the lowest 20 percent by both measures (table 5.7). The smallest mean benefits occur in the top income quintile. However, the target efficiency measures of tables 5.1 and 5.2 are lower than any of the other income-conditioned programs because substantial benefits are received by families in the middle quintile of both income and eco-

TABLE 5.7
Mean Veterans' Benefits by Current Income and Economic Welfare Measure

	Economic Welfare Measure					
	First Quintile	Second Quintile	Third Quintile	Fourth Quintile	Fifth Quintile	
Current Income						Total
First quintile	$187.93	$81.64	$ 39.43	$152.39	$65.57	$143.61
Second quintile	121.34	71.25	105.99	65.56	5.50	86.69
Third quintile	45.41	99.57	136.95	128.51	77.26	111.39
Fourth quintile	42.64	53.60	41.58	85.55	75.63	66.70
Fifth quintile	0	2.71	0	33.71	21.44	21.46
Total	147.74	77.06	82.21	83.77	41.57	86.47

nomic welfare. The similarities in the two distributions are striking and consistent with the target efficiency figures.

Unemployment Insurance and Workmen's Compensation

As the smallest of the cash transfers examined here, unemployment insurance and workmen's compensation are not very important to the aged. Transfers to this group provided 2.8 percent of aged families a mean of $348 in benefits. As table D.5 (p. 129) indicates, benefits are scattered across the entire income distribution, with the heaviest concentration of recipients at higher levels. There is no strong pattern for the size of recipient benefits. For the economic welfare measure, no families below the $1,000 level benefit from either of these programs. Above that level there is no consistent pattern to the percentage of recipients.

In table 5.8, benefits again display no particular pattern for income, while the two highest quintiles by the economic welfare measure capture a substantially large portion of the benefits. Certainly one reason for the lack of benefits to low income and low economic welfare families is that persons who might be unemployed for long periods of time are likely to retire and receive Social Security benefits rather than unemployment insurance. With this alternative, it may be that only higher income and welfare families are likely to remain in the labor force while unemployed. These families can afford to wait and probably have better prospects for regaining employment. These observations are also borne out by the low target efficiency measures. In all cases, the percentages of benefits to those at the bottom of the distributions are smaller than the percentages of families included in the group.

TABLE 5.8
Mean Unemployment and Workmen's Compensation Benefits by
Current Income and Economic Welfare Measure

	Economic Welfare Measure					
Current Income	First Quintile	Second Quintile	Third Quintile	Fourth Quintile	Fifth Quintile	Total
First quintile	$ 7.90	$4.44	$ 1.71	$ 0	$ 0	$ 5.89
Second quintile	4.07	6.70	2.50	51.13	16.65	10.03
Third quintile	18.39	2.33	.14	10.48	13.70	6.71
Fourth quintile	2.54	8.63	11.60	5.67	41.70	16.46
Fifth quintile	20.03	.60	1.29	5.02	12.62	9.27
Total	8.44	5.11	3.28	11.11	20.79	9.74

IN-KIND TRANSFERS

The three in-kind transfers estimated for this research together contribute more than $375 to the expanded measure of economic status. Medicare is treated as an insurance program which aids all aged persons, and is consequently the largest of the three. Medicaid is also implicitly an insurance program with a more restricted recipient population. Finally, public housing represents the smallest program studied, with benefits confined to a limited number of recipients.

Before the results are presented, the effect of treating Medicare and Medicaid as insurance programs deserves some attention. This approach enables identification of beneficiaries and avoids the problem of overstating the level of welfare of persons in ill health. However, such a diffusion of benefits underestimates the distributional impact of these programs. As discussed above, the Medicare program has been crudely adjusted for differences in utilization by income class. However, additional systematic biases (such as by race) have also been suggested. Unfortunately, it was not possible to incorporate into this research such adjustments for the medical programs.

Medicare

The Medicare program, as estimated here, provided mean benefits of $247.17 to each aged family. Since family benefits vary by income, family size, number of aged members, and region of residence, it is interesting to examine the distribution of benefits to identify any systematic differences. Table D.6 (p. 130) presents average recipient benefits by economic welfare and income class. Since all aged families are viewed as recipients, average benefits and recipient benefits are the same. For both current income and the expanded measure, the size of average benefits tends to increase at higher dollar levels.

While all aged families benefit from the program to some extent, Medicare is a rather inefficient way to raise the economic status of those at the bottom of the distribution. Target efficiency measures indicate, for example, that the 30 percent of families at the bottom of the distribution of economic welfare receive only about 26.6 percent of Medicare benefits (table 5.2). Although the Medicare program is not intended to concentrate on those at the bottom of the distribution, it is interesting to note that this group receives a less than proportional share of total benefits. Three observations help to explain this phenomenon. First, the benefit levels have been adjusted by money

TABLE 5.9
Mean Medicare Benefits by Current Income and Economic Welfare Measure

| Current Income | Economic Welfare Measure | | | | | |
	First Quintile	Second Quintile	Third Quintile	Fourth Quintile	Fifth Quintile	Total
First quintile	$205.13	$216.51	$230.32	$235.55	$240.08	$214.92
Second quintile	208.37	228.80	222.73	233.81	255.50	224.36
Third quintile	198.33	232.42	242.71	245.69	251.85	237.59
Fourth quintile	226.87	222.18	241.24	246.13	274.78	247.80
Fifth quintile	263.24	234.15	257.87	271.40	349.31	311.09
Total	207.84	227.43	238.87	250.96	310.15	247.17

income. However, the lowest income grouping—those under the $5,000 level—includes more than 60 percent of all aged families. This adjustment, then, cannot account for the discrepancies in the lowest three quintiles (and only part of the fourth) by income in table 5.9. The remaining differences can thus be attributed to family composition and region of residence. Aged families with minor children tend to be less well-off on the whole, and when the Medicare benefit is adjusted for family size, these families, who are often at the lower tail of the distribution, have lower benefits. Poorer aged families tend to live in regions, such as the South, which provide lower Medicare benefits.

Medicaid

As computed here, mean Medicaid benefits to the aged are less than half the size of mean Medicare benefits. However, for the 32 percent of aged families who are recipients, mean benefits of $346 are higher than those for Medicare. The Medicaid program is both asset- and income-conditioned, so most benefits should be confined to the lower portion of both the income and economic welfare distributions. Indeed, the mean benefits presented in table 5.10 show a concentration of recipients extending from the bottom of each distribution through the third quintile. A sizable number of recipients fall above the $1,970 poverty threshold (and hence into the third income quintile) because of the provisions for medically indigent families under Medicaid. Consequently, the target efficiency measures are also lower for Medicaid than for public assistance. The comparison between public assistance and Medicaid provides an excellent opportunity to examine the implications of the target efficiency measure. Public assistance ranks first by target efficiency, but does so by being a very re-

TABLE 5.10

Mean Medicaid Benefits by Current Income and Economic Welfare Measure

Current Income	Economic Welfare Measure					
	First Quintile	Second Quintile	Third Quintile	Fourth Quintile	Fifth Quintile	Total
First quintile	$245.16	$212.16	$202.70	$161.64	$201.27	$225.86
Second quintile	298.83	202.16	140.15	56.92	14.94	205.51
Third quintile	101.53	201.79	78.24	48.51	16.75	117.47
Fourth quintile	86.69	79.32	24.90	7.94	0	24.32
Fifth quintile	0	0	5.35	7.67	3.31	4.69
Total	240.20	182.51	78.18	31.89	13.48	115.45

strictive program. By the estimates used here, Medicaid expands that public assistance coverage to include other poor and near-poor families, and consequently suffers a dramatic decline in target efficiency.

The insurance treatment of the Medicaid program spreads benefits over a broad segment of the aged population—probably in a more generous fashion than occurs in practice. Indeed, those families in table 5.10 who rank lowest for both measures should be almost universally covered. Mean overall benefits in those cells closely resemble recipient benefit amounts at the bottom of each distribution in table D.7 (p. 131).

Public Housing

The public housing program represents the smallest transfer studied here. Only 1.28 percent of all aged families receive any benefits. Moreover, recipient benefits of $378 per family yield an overall average of only $4.84. Benefits from this program are heavily concentrated at the bottom of each distribution, although they are more dispersed for current money income. Recipients and their mean benefits are both substantially higher at lower levels of economic welfare (table D.8, p. 132).

The target efficiency of public housing is second only to public assistance (table 5.2, p. 88). The lowest 30 percent of all families receive 63.1 percent of benefits measured against current income and 83 percent when calculated for the measure of economic status. Moreover, there is an even greater discrepancy between the 15 percent target efficiency figures. The figures for current income reflect the common observation that while public housing is targeted at the poor

TABLE 5.11

Mean Public Housing Benefits by Current Income and Economic Welfare Measure

| | Economic Welfare Measure | | | | | |
Current Income	First Quintile	Second Quintile	Third Quintile	Fourth Quintile	Fifth Quintile	Total
First quintile	$20.09	$ 0	$0	$0	$0	$11.69
Second quintile	14.91	5.15	1.59	0	0	6.50
Third quintile	1.06	13.22	1.59	.32	0	4.75
Fourth quintile	.57	.47	2.18	1.04	0	.97
Fifth quintile	.91	.41	0	.33	.34	.31
Total	15.76	6.09	1.37	.53	.19	4.84

in general, the very poor within this group (measured by current income) benefit relatively less.[6] However, this criticism is not applicable when the distribution of economic welfare is used as the indicator of economic status. A large portion of the discrepancy between the two measures can be explained by the fact that the expanded measure includes the value of home equity. Since homeowners move up in the distribution relative to others with the same income, and since public housing recipients do not own their own homes, public housing is particularly target efficient by the economic welfare measure. Table 5.11 underscores this finding. Families whose economic status rankings increase when the expanded measure is used are seldom public housing recipients.

TAX EXPENDITURES

Tax expenditures provide benefits to aged families through a reduction in the income tax liability they would face without such tax provisions.[7] Although there are a large number of such tax transfers in the federal personal income tax, only the three most directly targeted at the aged have been estimated here. These include the double personal exemption for persons sixty-five and older, the retirement income tax credit, and the exclusion of Social Security and other public transfer income.

The benefit from each of these tax transfers is calculated as the difference between a family's tax liability and the liability which

[6] See, for example, Aaron (1972, p. 114) and Smolensky and Gomery (1973, pp. 172–73).

[7] See, for example, Surrey and Hellmuth (1969).

would exist without the particular tax expenditure. For example, to compute the incidence of the double personal exemption, tax liabilities are recalculated for each family *without* subtracting the additional $600 for each member over sixty-five. This amount should be greater than or equal to the tax liability computed with the exemption. When the tax liability with the exemption is subtracted from the liability without the exemption, a positive (or zero) benefit will result.

Double Personal Exemption

The first of the three tax transfers estimated here is the double personal exemption. In 1966, this provision allowed aged families to deduct from taxable income an additional $600 for each family member over sixty-five. Combined with the regular exemption and the standard deduction, the double exemption ensured that an aged couple would have no tax liability until their income exceeded $2,800. Estimated tax savings for this provision average $37.06 for all aged families and $130.64 for recipient families—who comprise 28.4 percent of the total. It is apparent from the quintile distribution for current income as well as economic welfare (the marginal totals in table 5.12) that the marginal benefits from the double personal exemption rise for higher quintiles. However, the increase is more dramatic for current income. For both measures, the percentage of families receiving benefits increases substantially. Recipient family benefits increase as money income rises. However, for the distribution of economic welfare, recipient benefits display a more complicated relationship between the income-conditioned tax transfer and the expanded economic status measure. The cause of the more gradual increase, and hence the higher target efficiency measures by economic welfare, is readily discernible from table 5.12. Those whose economic welfare ranking increases over income are in the upper right hand portion of the table. Although these families now have high levels of economic status, this is due to increases from sources that do not affect current income and, hence, income tax liability.

On the other hand, those who fall by economic welfare status from higher income rankings (lower left hand corner of the table) do so in large part because of the earnings adjustment. Families with large amounts of current earnings have those earnings reduced by the economic status measure as described earlier. Thus, while they may end up in the lowest quintile by the expanded measure, their incomes, tax liabilities, and hence, potential benefits from this tax expenditure remain high. This effect tends to equalize benefits from the double

TABLE 5.12

Mean Benefits from Double Personal Exemption by Current Income and
Economic Welfare Measure

	Economic Welfare Measure					
Current Income	First Quintile	Second Quintile	Third Quintile	Fourth Quintile	Fifth Quintile	Total
First quintile	$ 0	$ 0	$ 0	$ .16	$ 0	$ .01
Second quintile	.75	.80	.10	.09	.73	.58
Third quintile	20.27	3.77	1.33	4.44	4.67	4.48
Fourth quintile	117.28	78.25	34.76	35.24	28.10	43.19
Fifth quintile	160.31	144.81	138.50	135.22	136.70	137.28
Total	12.13	15.86	24.77	51.95	81.99	37.06

exemption by quintile rankings of the economic welfare measure. The
tax benefits still show an upward trend since part of earnings and all
other taxable income sources contribute positively to economic
welfare.

Exclusion of Transfer Income

While the tax provision which allows for the exclusion of Social
Security, Railroad Retirement, public assistance, and certain other
public transfer income is not limited to the aged, the elderly form the
principal beneficiary group. Estimated mean benefits to the aged from
this program total $77.61—a figure nearly as high as public assistance
benefits. Actual recipients comprise 40.6 percent of the families and
receive benefits of $190.70 on average. Table D.10 (p. 134) shows
benefits by welfare and income class. The percentage of recipients and
their average benefits tend to rise across the distribution, although the
trend is not as pronounced as for the double exemption. For income,
there is a substantial jump in the percent of recipients above the
$2,000 level that reaches a peak for the $4,000 class.

While persons with higher incomes receive larger tax savings
from Social Security income because of their higher tax brackets, not
all these families have such transfer income. Thus, coverage at higher
incomes is less universal than for the double exemption. Moreover, for
money income, benefits do not begin until an even higher dollar class
than that for the double exemption, reflecting the fact that tax
liabilities for these families are so low that they do not benefit from
both the double exemption and the exclusion of transfer income. Although the target efficiency rankings place the double exemption

TABLE 5.13
Mean Benefits from Exclusion of Transfer Payments from Taxable Income
by Current Income and Economic Welfare Measure

| | Economic Welfare Measure | | | | | |
| | First Quintile | Second Quintile | Third Quintile | Fourth Quintile | Fifth Quintile | Total |
Current Income						
First quintile	$ 0	$ 0	$ 0	$ 0	$ 0	$ 0
Second quintile	.20	.26	.47	.22	.24	.28
Third quintile	21.96	24.53	28.99	25.85	29.95	26.57
Fourth quintile	89.09	92.98	112.26	130.06	112.47	114.55
Fifth quintile	92.99	89.09	176.45	225.57	291.65	246.08
Total	8.76	21.91	61.47	116.21	189.12	77.50

above the exclusion of transfer income, this latter tax transfer would target a higher percentage of total benefits to middle income (and economic welfare) families. Thus, here is a case where establishing a preference between these two tax transfers might require more distributional information. The same relationship between income and welfare rankings as described for the double exemption explains why target efficiencies are larger for the expanded measure (table 5.13) than for current income.

Retirement Income Tax Credit

The third and smallest tax provision is the retirement income tax credit. This provision reduces tax liability once it has been computed rather than altering taxable income. To some extent it serves as a complementary provision to the exclusion of transfer income by allowing a credit against otherwise taxable pension and interest income. However, this credit also excludes earnings. Families at the upper end of the income distribution receive the highest concentration of benefits. To qualify for this credit, families must have incomes that exceed both the usual exemptions allowed and the two other tax expenditures described here. Moreover, the aged family must have property, pension, or annuity income. Only then can an elderly family benefit from this tax expenditure. As Table D.11 (p. 135) indicates, only families above the $2,000 level of current income qualify. Although participation rises by income class, it covers no more than 37 percent of families even at the highest income level. Consequently, this tax transfer provides benefits to just 9 percent of aged families, averaging $14.56 overall. The $162.80 benefit to the recipient families is larger than

TABLE 5.14

Mean Benefits from Retirement Income Tax Credit by Current Income and Economic Welfare Measure

	Economic Welfare Measure					
Current Income	First Quintile	Second Quintile	Third Quintile	Fourth Quintile	Fifth Quintile	Total
First quintile	$ 0	$0	$ 0	$ 0	$ 0	$ 0
Second quintile	0	0	0	0	0	0
Third quintile	.36	1.61	.73	3.07	1.89	1.52
Fourth quintile	14.13	4.74	7.07	8.19	13.87	9.19
Fifth quintile	1.77	2.68	21.13	34.13	91.35	62.14
Total	.89	1.09	4.50	13.17	53.89	14.56

recipient benefits for the double exemption, but few aged families are able to obtain it. Thus, this transfer is not only least likely to benefit any poor aged families, it is also of very limited application even at higher income and welfare levels.

As shown in table 5.14, a portion of the benefits from this tax expenditure go to those in the lower quintiles by the economic welfare measure. Again, this is because some families with high money incomes fall into lower quintiles when the expanded measure of economic status is used. However, average benefits are particularly large for the highest quintile by both measures. Families with substantial property income are likely to have large annuities and thus to benefit from the retirement income tax credit. Moreover, since earnings are excluded from this credit, fewer families with high incomes but low economic welfare receive this benefit.

TRANSFER BENEFITS BY DEMOGRAPHIC GROUP

Just as the benefits from transfers and tax expenditures vary by income and welfare class, they also differ by demographic characteristics for aged families. Race, sex, and even age breakdowns for head of family reveal more about the impact of government transfers. Table 5.15 disaggregates average benefits for five of the programs by various demographic characteristics. For age, race, and sex, Social Security and public assistance seem to vary in opposite directions. Families headed by persons in their seventies, whites, and males receive the highest Social Security benefits but relatively low assistance payments. In fact, public assistance appears to play a complementary role to the larger Social Security program. The other two income-conditioned transfers, Medicaid and public housing, also vary closely with public assistance except for the youngest age group.

As Davis and Reynolds (1973) and Holahan (1975) point out, actual medical reimbursements to nonwhites are systematically lower in the Medicare and Medicaid programs. In table 5.15 the estimations of the insurance values do yield lower benefits for nonwhites for Medicare, but the magnitude of the differences is probably larger than that captured here. Moreover, the Medicaid estimates indicate higher benefits for nonwhite families. Such families are implicitly assumed to have equal access to medical care and hence equal insurance benefits. A more sensitive insurance calculation for these programs should correct the results to reflect the actual lower access to medical care by nonwhites.

The age distribution within aged families also contains some interesting results. Families headed by persons in their seventies receive the largest total transfers, mainly because of high Social Security benefits. These families have few labor force participants, which qualifies them for Social Security and other transfers. In addition, they are likely to have better coverage from Social Security than the older, eighty-and-above group. The low benefits to those over eighty may improve as cohorts who are more fully covered reach that age.

A second view of benefits by demographic group concentrates on

TABLE 5.15
Mean Transfer Benefits by Demographic Characteristics

Characteristic	Social Security	Public Assistance	Medicare	Medicaid	Public Housing
Race of head					
White	$1124.24	$ 68.20	$250.49	$108.28	$ 3.38
Nonwhite	812.73	209.04	210.69	192.47	21.00
Age of head					
18–64	842.39	44.93	255.01	226.59	0.15
65–69	990.91	44.87	233.33	71.60	4.61
70–74	1287.28	79.85	258.57	89.10	8.05
75–79	1283.11	84.91	267.66	101.70	3.82
80–99	998.62	177.87	251.38	152.24	5.89
Sex of head					
Female	881.34	131.67	233.96	141.79	9.41
Male	1214.82	52.15	259.68	101.02	2.39
Work status					
No aged workers	1154.20	104.45	237.88	146.00	6.46
One or more workers	974.81	25.95	267.75	47.54	1.28

the lowest two quintiles of the income and economic welfare distributions. The figures given in table 5.16 are ratios of the share of benefits to the proportion of families with a particular characteristic who comprise the lowest 40 percent of aged families by current income. The proportion of families with certain characteristics may vary for different transfers because the distribution net of the transfer studied must be recomputed each time. Table 5.17 presents the same ratios but is based on the economic welfare measure. Thus, in table 5.17 the Social Security ratio for female-headed families is .788. Female heads comprise 46 percent of the bottom two quintiles but receive only 36.25 percent of the Social Security benefits available to those quintiles. Again, the results are limited to five of the transfer programs: Social Security, public assistance, and the three in-kind transfers.

On the whole, the discrepancies by demographic characteristics for the lowest 40 percent of each distribution vary in the same fashion as mean benefits. That is, mean Social Security benefits are substantially higher for families where the head is white. In both tables 5.16 and 5.17 the ratios also diverge, with nonwhites in the lowest two quintiles receiving a less than proportional share of these benefits which accrue to those two quintiles. Whites also receive greater than

TABLE 5.16
Ratio of Benefits to Recipients as Proportion of
Lowest Two Quintiles of Current Income

Characteristic	Social Security	Public Assistance	Medicare	Medicaid	Public Housing
Race of head					
White	1.048	.906	1.017	.991	.684
Nonwhite	.623	1.583	.895	1.055	2.959
Age of head					
18–64	.760	.287	1.009	1.261	.023
65–69	1.073	.928	.889	.871	1.386
70–74	1.156	1.290	.969	.967	2.350
75–79	1.134	1.091	1.071	.854	.683
80–99	.943	1.579	1.052	.964	.876
Sex of head					
Female	.984	1.179	.952	.903	1.338
Male	1.012	.817	1.050	1.101	.648
Work Status					
No aged workers	1.000	1.049	.998	1.031	1.068
One or more workers	.997	.614	1.016	.759	.478

TABLE 5.17
Ratio of Benefits to Recipients as Proportion of Lowest
Two Quintiles of Economic Welfare Measure

Characteristic	Social Security	Public Assistance	Medicare	Medicaid	Public Housing
Race of head					
White	1.049	.912	1.016	.994	.775
Nonwhite	.709	1.492	.908	1.036	2.263
Age of head					
18–64	.806	.391	.975	1.196	.029
65–69	1.007	.647	.915	.735	.883
70–74	1.107	1.092	1.019	.948	1.954
75–79	1.089	1.176	1.082	1.045	.855
80–99	.828	1.938	1.045	1.246	1.075
Sex of head					
Female	.788	1.232	1.206	1.030	1.465
Male	1.181	.779	.868	.972	.565
Work status					
No aged workers	1.015	1.194	1.005	1.124	1.202
One or more workers	.941	.282	.982	.543	.274

proportional shares of Medicare but a lower share of the income-conditioned transfers. The same generalization also applies to male heads of families for the income distribution, with the exception of the Medicaid program. Family heads in their seventies also fare better, as do families with no labor force participants.

A comparison of the ratios for the income and economic welfare distributions shows little variation by race. However, the ratios change substantially by sex of head and, to a lesser extent, by age and work status. Female family heads receive a greater than proportional share of both Medicare and Medicaid. Families headed by older persons (seventy-five and above) and with no aged labor force participants tend to receive higher proportional shares by the economic welfare measure. It is no coincidence that these three groups—families with female heads, older heads, and no labor force participants—also show greater relative gains when ranked by the expanded measure of economic status. Families with access to additional resources who subsequently improve their status are less likely to receive transfer payments. Consequently, the families with that demographic characteristic, who also remain in the bottom 40 percent by the expanded measure, are more often transfer recipients.

CONCLUSION

Government pensions, workmen's compensation, and unemployment benefits do provide substantial benefits to some aged families. However, government pensions are available only to former government employees covered by the program. Although it aids those families, it is, by definition, a very restricted transfer. The small size of workmen's compensation and unemployment results in the lowest ranking for the economic welfare distribution in table 5.3. Social Security and Medicare provide almost universal coverage for the aged but are a very inefficient way of helping those at the lower end of both distributions. Medicare actually provides less than proportional benefits to this group. While these programs certainly aid the poor, viewing Social Security increases as a means of raising more people above poverty is at best an indirect approach. Moreover, although not explored here, the interrelationships between government programs are crucial to this issue. In the past, for example, aged recipients of both Social Security and public assistance have experienced a fully offsetting decline in OAA when Social Security payments have risen.

The income-conditioned transfers which provide the greatest share of benefits to aged families with the lowest resource levels are nonetheless of limited help to this group. They have high target efficiencies, in part because of the stringency of their requirements. Consequently, even for those at the very lowest income and welfare levels coverage is not universal. The limited nature of these transfers is also reflected in table 5.3, which ranks programs by their dollar contributions to aged families. Particularly for the lowest 40 percent of these families the rankings are low. However, Medicaid fares better in this instance because the estimation procedure to determine the insurance values yields more comprehensive coverage of families. If Medicaid (and other programs) actually provided benefits as they are estimated here, more of the aged poor would receive transfers. One additional possibility should be explored further: it is not known how many families eligible for but not receiving benefits choose not to participate. This would probably result in lower target efficiency figures. There seems to be a tradeoff between more comprehensive coverage of the target group and more exclusion of benefits to those outside the target group.

The tax expenditures estimated here are, on the whole, the most inefficient means for directing resources toward the aged poor. To receive benefits, the aged family must pay income taxes. In every instance, more than 40 percent of all benefits from each of these programs are directed at the highest 20 percent of families by either distribution. If one or more of these programs were eliminated, it would improve the target efficiency of the remaining tax transfers. That is, these programs are generally redundant for most aged families. The existence of the double personal exemption (in conjunction with other "standard" exemptions) could eliminate the liability for most families. The exemption of transfer income is unnecessary for any aged couple with an income under $2,800.

The effect of government transfers on families at the bottom of the distributions is strikingly similar for both the current income and economic welfare measures. In determining eligibility for income-conditioned transfers, nonincome sources of economic welfare are considered. Beneficiaries of the remaining transfers tend to be randomly distributed such that the number who rise by economic status just about offset the number who decline. Consequently, the distribution of benefits changes little between the two measures.

6

Policy Implications and Future Directions

This study derives a measure of economic welfare for aged families and examines the distributional impact of various government programs on families ranked by the measure of economic welfare and by current income. In so doing, the research makes some important contributions and establishes a basis for future study. This chapter briefly mentions some of these contributions and their policy implications and then suggests possible directions for future research.

SIGNIFICANCE OF THE ECONOMIC WELFARE MEASURE

The measure of economic welfare as defined here is consistent with a life-cycle hypothesis of savings, and attempts to capture a yearly level of potential consumption for each aged family. Among the estimated components included are adjusted earnings, private pensions, a share of the family's total net worth, intrafamily transfers, and cash and in-kind transfers net of payroll and income taxes. Although the value of leisure time is not measured, some of the theoretical issues concerning its estimate are discussed in chapter 2. The share of assets allocated to consumption each year is based on assumptions about the lifetime utility function, the stability of other components over time, the interest rate, and the family's life expectancy.

This research has drawn on the work of a number of others, including Weisbrod and Hansen, Taussig, and Morgan et al. However, it is the only study that specifically focuses on the aged and, as such, provides a comprehensive measure of well-being for this important subgroup. In an additional departure from earlier studies, consumer theory provides the basis for the measure, dictating the form of the resources included. Finally, three of the estimation techniques developed here differ substantially from any used in previous research, and hence deserve particular attention.

Earnings are adjusted downward for aged workers. Since it is assumed that families wish to maintain a stable level of consumption over time and that workers will participate in the labor force for only part of their remaining lifetimes, a life-cycle approach requires that not all of current earnings be applied to present consumption. The adjustment procedure used leaves only a portion of earnings—corresponding to expected income replacement from other sources—as part of the cash component of economic status. The remaining amount, multiplied by years of expected future labor-force participation, is spread over the entire lifetime of the worker. Implicitly, this is comparable to keeping earnings intact but providing a smaller current annuity which would increase upon the worker's retirement by an amount just sufficient to offset lost income. By accounting for future expected earnings, this measure avoids the age bias that would result from a constant annuity treatment for net worth.

A second notable estimation technique also concerns the annuity calculation. The treatment of home equity incorporates an adjustment to reflect difficulties of liquidating this asset. An elderly family is assumed to purchase an annuity on that portion of its home which would remain after the death of the last aged member. This annuity plus the rental services of the house during the family's lifetime total less than reported home equity. The difference, termed an insurance reduction, is calculated and subtracted from the reported value of home equity. Thus, a family with liquid assets totaling the same amount as the home equity of a second family will receive a higher current annuity, since liquid assets are more readily consumed. Again, this technique avoids one of the criticisms leveled against including net worth in a measure of economic status.

The estimate for intrafamily transfers is also unique. This is a particularly unresearched area, even though such transfers represent an important determinant of the well-being of the aged. For the 30 percent of elderly families who reside with other relatives in extended family units, a simple formula approximates the benefits (or costs) from such living arrangements using the limited available information. Although the measure is, of necessity, somewhat arbitrary, it yields striking results that do not vary substantially even when upper- or lower-bound estimates are substituted. Aged couples or individuals who reside in larger extended family groups fall at the extremes of the income distribution. The income levels of their younger relatives tend to fall at the opposite extremes. Consequently, when transfers are introduced into the measure, they exhibit a strong equalizing effect.

The usual specification of aged families as those headed by someone over sixty-five ignores the aged who reside with younger relatives. This latter group is strongly concentrated at lower income levels, but their positions improve when intrafamily transfers are calculated. Without the adjustment in the definition of "aged family" so as to include families with an elderly member, an intrafamily transfer estimate would suggest that benefits in extended family groups flow from the old to the young. Thus, the definition of "aged family" becomes quite important to the ultimate distribution of economic status.

The specification of family composition used here results in a lower income distribution than does the standard specification, which includes income from the younger family members. When the net worth annuity replaces property income, the average dollar amount to each family rises but the distribution becomes more skewed. The addition of in-kind transfers also has a substantial positive effect on the distribution, largely as a result of the assumption that all aged families receive Medicare benefits. On the other hand, the inclusion of tax liabilities leaves the economic status of most families at the bottom of the distribution unchanged. The median does fall as families at higher economic status levels incur the tax liabilities. Intrafamily transfers reduce both tails of the distribution and raise the median slightly.

Thus, the economic welfare measure has a more equal distribution, a higher median value, and in general lies to the right of the distribution of current income. More important, the ranking of aged families within each distribution varies substantially. Families do not uniformly benefit from the additional resources incorporated into the economic status measure; indeed, some families fall both by rank and by dollar class. Families with aged workers exhibit, on average, lower dollar values for the economic status measure than they do when current income is used. In contrast, families headed by persons over eighty years of age or by women show relatively large gains when their economic status is based on the expanded measure. For older families, the life expectancy variable in the annuity calculation ensures such a result. However, it may also indicate that actual consumption by most aged families is lower than the measure allows, perhaps because of a bequest motive. If so, aged families would dissave less each year and consequently retain higher levels of net worth over time. Gains in economic status by women reflect the high proportion of widows residing with their children and sharing in their resources. Also, few women participate in the labor force after age sixty-five. Consequently, women are less likely to fall by rank when earnings are adjusted. Finally, as mentioned above, when the elderly reside with younger relatives, their level of economic status can shift substantially in either direction according to the degree of their dependence on those relatives.

These findings provide much valuable information about the aged. It has long been asserted that nonincome sources of well-being are important for this group. This study identifies both the absolute size and the equalizing (or "disequalizing") effect of in-kind transfers, net worth, taxes, and intrafamily transfers. Moreover, an expanded measure of economic status such as the one developed here is better able to address issues of horizontal and vertical equity than is current income. Families with the same current income do not possess equal command over goods and services if they have unequal access to other resources. The level of net worth, eligibility for in-kind transfers, and living arrangements are all determinants of consumption possibilities for aged families. Since none of these are adequately captured by money income, that indicator of economic status cannot guarantee the identification of "equals." In addition, as shown in chapter 4, the rank ordering of families changes when nonincome components are included in the measure. Vertical equity—the ranking of families by level of economic status—thus may also be misstated by current income.

The measure captures the level of consumption a family could expect to maintain over its remaining lifetime rather than over one year only. It underscores the permanent low resource position faced by a substantial minority of the population. Those in the bottom one or two quintiles by both the income *and* economic welfare measures are not only currently poor but also have few prospects for improvement. This large number of the elderly whose positions remain virtually unchanged when more resources are taken into account provides dramatic evidence of the need for stable, continuing support programs for at least a portion of elderly families.

After computing the distribution of economic welfare, the rankings of families by this measure and by the distribution of money income are used to gauge the effectiveness of government programs. Of particular concern are the benefits accruing to families at the bottom of each distributional ranking. Results from this part of the research provide information on eleven existing government programs by both money income and economic welfare measures, and present a unique opportunity for comparisons.

A measure which captures horizontal and vertical equity is better equipped to assess the distributional effects of various transfer (or other redistributional) programs. Discrepancies in the target efficiency figures of chapter 5 result because of differences in the composition of families ranked at the bottom of each distribution. Thus, for example, current income estimates rate public housing 25 percentage points below the target efficiency figures for the economic welfare measure. This is a consequence of the fact that the benefits of home ownership are not captured in current income. When these homeowners rise in rank order relative to their nonhomeowning counterparts by the economic welfare measure, public housing becomes a more target efficient program.

Actually, the surprising finding of this study is that target efficiency estimates change so little between the two measures. There are two principal reasons. First, income-conditioned programs also tend to have strict requirements about assets and contributions from relatives. Thus, they are target efficient by either measure. Certainly this is not a startling conclusion. However, it does underscore the ability of existing programs to exclude aged families with nonincome resources. Perhaps the more important issue in this context is whether the achievement of high vertical target efficiency necessitates the exclusion of many families who should receive benefits. For example, only 53 percent of those in the lowest quintile by both measures receive public assistance benefits. An explanation for the stability of the target efficiency measures for other programs requires some speculation. The size of benefits and percentage of beneficiaries seem to be randomly distributed by income and welfare class. Thus, a reshuffling of the families at the bottom of the distribution produces few effects.

Social Security appears to be a neutral per capita distributional program for both status measures. The minimum floor on benefits offsets the higher average amounts paid to a smaller percentage of those at higher income and welfare levels. Nonetheless, in absolute dollars, Social Security provides the largest transfers to the elderly poor.

Medicare, Medicaid, and unemployment insurance are relatively ineffective in aiding families at the lower tail of the distribution. Not only do they fail to direct large proportions of their benefits to those at the bottom of each distribution, but at the time of the OEO survey they were also limited in scope as well. Public assistance, public housing, and perhaps veterans' benefits could be cited as particularly helpful to the aged poor, yet altogether they total only a little over $2 billion of the more than $26 billion paid by all the programs studied here. Again, they may appear to be so target efficient because they exclude many families who may or may not be eligible. Finally, families at the upper end of both the economic welfare and income distributions receive the heaviest concentration of tax expenditure benefits. The personal exemptions and standard deductions available to all taxpayers combined with only one of the tax expenditures would fully exempt large numbers of the aged from income tax liability. Hence for all but the highest income elderly, one or two of these "aged" tax expenditures are unnecessary.

FUTURE DIRECTIONS

The research undertaken here establishes a first step towards a more comprehensive measure of economic welfare for the aged. A great deal remains to be done, both in refining the measure for the aged and in extending it to other groups. The following sections suggest some possible directions for future research.

Improving the Measure

Improvement in the measure of economic status for the aged requires better survey data. Not only is the SEO now somewhat dated, but the drawbacks mentioned in earlier chapters limit its usefulness. Many government programs originate or are administered at the state level; even the federal Medicare program yields differential benefits by state. Thus, the identification of a family's state of residence would allow better estimates of the transfer programs included in the SEO. In addition, more specific in-kind information is necessary. Although the Food Stamp program was still quite small in 1967, any updated survey should certainly contain data on this transfer. A new data source should also generate better asset information and a more careful delineation of income and asset breakdowns by nuclear families residing in larger units. Finally, a good accounting of health status, reasons for retirement, and current use of leisure time could aid researchers seeking to estimate the value of leisure and non-market-productive activities and to better adjust for family needs.

If all the variables from chapter 2 could be included in the measure of economic status, they would surely alter its distribution. The largest exclusion, the value of leisure time, would place families with labor force participants at a further disadvantage and hence tend to equalize the distribution. Moreover, if the researcher could differentiate between those who are voluntarily and involuntarily retired, the resulting variations in the estimated values would have a substantive effect on horizontal equity. Those who enjoy their leisure would no longer have a level of economic welfare comparable to that of families with similar resources who prefer to work. Since many of those involuntarily retired have low current incomes and insufficient other resources which prevent them from utilizing their leisure time, a sensitive estimate of the value of leisure would be likely to increase the inequality among retired families. Thus, the overall effect on the measure is uncertain.

The second major source of exclusion concerns government taxes and expenditures. The measure of chapter 3 includes on balance more expenditure than taxation items. Consequently if the total impact of government were included, the absolute level of measured economic status would fall. Changes in the equality of the distribution are more difficult to predict. As pointed out in chapter 3, the omitted taxes do not seem to be very redistributive. They are only slightly regressive (when measured against current income). Those portions of government spending considered public goods are also thought *not* to be redistributive. Omitted in-kind transfers could affect a few individual families substantially, but were too small in 1966 to alter greatly the distribution of economic welfare.

Finally, economists know that transfers among relatives occur even when an extended unit is not involved. A better measure of these family transfers, particularly those made in kind, could also have a substantial effect on a small number of families. As was the case with intrafamily transfers estimated here, families at the extremes of the distribution are the more likely donors or recipients. Thus, it might be expected that improvements in the measure as suggested here would largely yield more reliable welfare estimates for individual families or particular demographic groups, rather than drastically change the overall level of measured economic status.

An updated estimation of the economic status measure would be of interest even if all the improvements discussed here were not possible. Since 1966, a number of important changes in the well-being of the aged have occurred. The Supplemental Security Income program replaced Old Age Assistance, and benefits under the Social Security program have been expanded.

Private pension programs continue to grow, and the age of retirement appears to be still declining. Thus the measure of economic status is likely to be quite different from what it was in 1966. Moreover, an update of the measure would permit comparisons with the improvement in income position that has occurred over time for the aged. Both relative and absolute definitions of poverty need to be developed for use with an expanded measure of economic status.

Extending the Welfare Measure

An entirely different approach to measuring economic welfare could be estimated to supplement and contrast with the status measure used here. Such an indicator would convert all current flows of resources to aged families into stocks. The computation of the asset value of Social Security and other pensions would treat current payments as annuities. Similar calculations could likewise convert other resources into a stock of net assets available to each family over its remaining lifetime.

A comparison of the ranking of aged families by such an indicator with the ranking from the measure used here would be particularly interesting. The measure of chapters 2 and 3 dictates that, for two families identical except for their life expectancies, the family with the lower life expectancy will be "better off" in the current time period. Indeed, the breakdown of economic status by age of family head (chapter 4) illustrates the extent to which such families improve their well-being over a current income measure. Such a result occurs because assets are allocated over the expected lifetime of the family, and a lower life expectancy allows the share of assets to be greater in any one year. Just the opposite bias exists for the alternative "stock" measure. When current annuities (such as Social Security) are converted to assets, the value to a family expected to live longer will be higher. Thus, a comparison of the two measures could contribute insights about the sensitivity of each to the life expectancy bias.

Abstracting from the aged, a comprehensive measure of economic welfare is desirable for other groups of the population as well. Even with the same theoretical basis, however, the conceptual and estimation problems would be quite different. For example, for families headed by young workers (i.e., aged thirty to forty), it might not be difficult to estimate the value of leisure time and non-market-productive activities. However, the stability of current resources over time, particularly the pattern of expected future earnings, might be very troublesome to predict for this group. Consequently, establishing the appropriate sign and size of the net worth share would pose considerable problems. Further work in the area would, however, allow better intergenerational comparisons of families than are now possible with current money income. A life-cycle measure removes the age bias inherent in an income measure of economic status. Again, this should lead to improvements in establishing vertical and horizontal equity. Moreover, a life-cycle measure would be particularly valuable for analyzing policy changes that alter family behavior over time. For example, when programs for the elderly change, the effects on potential future recipients may be of as much interest as those on current recipients. Could we expect a resulting change in savings behavior or family composition that would shift the incidence of the program? A permanent income approach for all families could handle such questions and help to estimate the actual incidence of policy changes.

Research on the economic status of the aged and on measures of economic welfare has been infrequent and incomplete. This study has dealt with both of these issues as well as with the distributional impact of government programs. No previous research has attempted to analyze all eleven programs examined here, nor combined a thorough study of the economic welfare of aged families with the impact of government programs on that welfare. However, a great deal of additional study is necessary to fill the remaining gaps in our knowledge.

APPENDIX A

Imputing Values for Missing Net Worth Data

To impute values for missing home equity and other net worth, multiple linear regressions were run using socioeconomic characteristics from families for whom asset information was intact. The coefficients obtained from the regressions are then used to predict net worth for families where it is not available. Home equity and the remaining components of net worth are estimated separately, so that the "insurance reduction" calculation can be made for home equity. Moreover, net worth for renters is estimated in a separate regression from that for homeowners. Thus, three estimates are calculated for families headed by an aged person and three more for families headed by a younger adult.

The independent variables attempt to capture those socioeconomic characteristics which would help to explain the resources a family has (or previously had) available for savings or the potential drain on resources from family needs. The variables include (1) the dividend, rental, and interest income of the family or individual, (2) current earnings, (3) Social Security payments, (4) education of the family head, (5) race of the family head, (6) size of family, (7) urban or rural location, (8) age and age-squared of the head, (9) region of residence, and (10) whether the family owns a farm. Overall, the most important variables are asset income, education, earnings, Social Security for those sixty-five and over, and the variable representing farm ownership. Region of residence is also important for the home equity estimates.

As mentioned in chapter 3, this procedure restricts the variance of both the additional imputations and the total estimates of net worth. If the missing data were distributed in the same manner as available data, then the variance of home equity and net worth would be the same for both the distribution of available values and the distribution of all families (where missing data are imputed). To achieve such a result, a random number is added to each imputed value to increase the variance of these estimates. The random numbers generated for this procedure are normally distributed with a variance equal to the standard error of the estimate from each regression equation.

APPENDIX B

Calculating the Economic Welfare Measure for Young Families

In order to compute intrafamily transfers for the aged, it is also necessary to derive an estimate of the "pre-intrafamily-transfer" level of economic welfare for the young subfamily of an extended family group. The estimation problems are similar to those discussed for aged families because, with some exceptions and modifications, the same components are used for this group.[1] Medicare, Social Security, and other pensions are assumed to benefit only the aged. The annuity value of net worth is attributed to the younger subfamily only when the head is under sixty-five and not the spouse of an aged person. When necessary, missing asset data are imputed as stated in Appendix A for these younger families.

Although Medicaid benefits are included in the measure for young families, the computations treat these families as a separate insurance group. The same formula is used to calculate benefits, but the insurance values to young families are much smaller than those for the aged since fewer payments are spread across a larger eligible population (see table B.1). Calculations per child are also included in the table; when minor children are the dependents of the aged members (i.e., no other younger adults are present), these estimates are included as the children's share of Medicaid benefits.

---

[1] To be totally correct, or if the measure were to be used to reflect the actual level of well-being for all young families, some of the computations would have to be adjusted. For example, S_t should not be a constant annuity if $\hat{Y}_t$ is expected to change over time. Young families might expect $\hat{Y}_t$ (especially the earnings portion) to rise and then fall.

The distribution of economic welfare for these younger families is shown in Appendix C.

TABLE B.1
Medicaid Computations for Young Families

Region	Insurance Benefits to Public Assistance Recipients	
	Benefits per Person	Benefits per Child
Northeast	$ 69.38	$ 54.49
North Central	53.92	41.64
West	140.80	111.38
South	30.33	21.04
	Insurance Benefits to the Medically Indigent	
Northeast	$119.07	$41.52
North Central	52.27	18.07
West	85.73	37.49
South	12.23	3.71

APPENDIX C

The Distribution of Economic Welfare for Young Families

Calculations for the economic welfare of the young subfamilies of extended family units yield the distributions shown in table C.1. The distributions are measured in equivalency units for a family of four. Thus, the median dollar level should be relatively high and can be gauged against the Orshansky poverty threshold of $3,345 (for a non-farm family of four in 1966). The median of $6,633 is equivalent to a welfare ratio of 1.98, and can be compared to the 1.93 welfare ratio for the median aged family in the final distribution of chapter 4. It should be noted, however, that the sample of young families used here includes only those with older relatives present in the household and should not be taken as representative of the younger population.

A comparison of the two distributions in table C.1 illustrates the influence of intrafamily transfers on the young subfamily. The same suppression of the extremes of the distribution occurs as was found for the older subfamilies. Incorporating intrafamily transfers into the distribution reduces the number of young subfamilies with incomes under $3,345 by 7 percentage points. Those at the bottom of the distribution tend to reside with relatives who are able to provide additional resources, while just the opposite is the case for the young families at the upper end.

TABLE C.1
Distribution of Economic Welfare Measures for Young Families

Dollar Values	Distribution of Welfare before Calculating Intrafamily Transfers	Percentage Distribution of Economic Welfare
Negative	.41%	.17%
$ 0	0	0
1–499	8.73	.17
500–999	3.43	.57
1000–1499	3.63	2.12
1500–1999	2.77	3.93
2000–2499	3.37	3.78
2500–2999	2.05	5.59
3000–3999	6.65	8.86
4000–4999	7.39	9.22
5000–5999	6.98	9.51
6000–7999	15.87	19.21
8000–9999	12.60	15.56
10,000–14,999	16.87	15.22
15,000 or more	9.25	6.09
Percent under $3345	26.68	19.39
Median	$6578	$6633
Mean	$7393.32	$7394.65

APPENDIX D

Benefits from Government Programs for Aged Families

The following tables present the percentage of families in each income and welfare class who receive benefits from a particular program and the average amount of benefits accruing to these recipients. These benefits differ from the figures presented in chapter 5, which calculate the average across all aged families. Table D.6 employs a different format since all aged families are assumed to be recipients of Medicare.

TABLE D.1
Distribution of Social Security Benefits

Dollar Values	By Current Income		By Economic Welfare Measure	
	Percentage Receiving Benefits	Average Benefit per Recipient Family	Percentage Receiving Benefits	Average Benefit per Recipient Family
Negative	85.73%	$1410.54	74.58%	$1558.49
$ 0	87.53	1201.15	—	—
1–499	87.88	1362.12	94.39	1219.59
500–999	86.21	1357.52	89.85	1395.24
1000–1499	85.13	1374.52	85.23	1281.08
1500–1999	85.78	1429.31	82.89	1269.50
2000–2499	83.02	1472.28	79.55	1338.12
2500–2999	86.08	1468.34	83.33	1319.73
3000–3999	79.45	1454.56	80.94	1376.38
4000–4999	68.82	1331.04	78.78	1323.54
5000–5999	62.24	1307.22	71.53	1450.27
6000–7999	58.37	1267.77	74.95	1422.66
8000–9999	50.51	1224.85	79.39	1408.07
10,000–14,999	60.26	1551.37	80.92	1578.24
15,000 or more	34.98	1411.26	76.71	1429.22
All families	81.11	1353.95	81.11	1353.95

TABLE D.2
Distribution of Public Assistance Benefits

Dollar Values	By Current Income		By Economic Welfare Measure	
	Percentage Receiving Benefits	Average Benefit per Recipient Family	Percentage Receiving Benefits	Average Benefit per Recipient Family
Negative	18.08%	$ 929.70	26.58%	$1072.06
$ 0	62.65	968.73	—	—
1–499	34.94	849.76	68.04	1009.85
500–999	32.06	726.25	62.51	1025.57
1000–1499	12.14	606.51	38.54	781.19
1500–1999	3.21	527.66	28.81	744.29
2000–2499	2.74	556.25	14.07	738.89
2500–2999	1.25	491.16	9.27	573.86
3000–3999	1.16	391.19	4.22	582.37
4000–4999	.95	581.06	1.52	674.13
5000–5999	.74	1335.64	2.57	469.27
6000–7999	.82	862.37	.84	746.94
8000–9999	1.16	507.41	.29	666.52
10,000–14,999	0	0	.19	1445.94
15,000 or more	0	0	0	0
All families	10.29	783.58	10.29	783.58

TABLE D.3
Distribution of Government Pension Benefits

Dollar Values	By Current Income		By Economic Welfare Measure	
	Percentage Receiving Benefits	Average Benefit per Recipient Family	Percentage Receiving Benefits	Average Benefit per Recipient Family
Negative	2.15%	$ 725.06	14.73%	$8400.00
$ 0	21.00	2647.43	—	—
1–499	14.79	3069.83	51.62	2334.68
500–999	12.94	2190.68	17.60	2762.21
1000–1499	13.87	1576.46	13.47	1953.84
1500–1999	10.35	1432.72	9.52	1381.96
2000–2499	9.39	2066.81	10.35	1803.92
2500–2999	7.97	1290.67	11.90	1798.58
3000–3999	10.51	2096.64	8.91	1577.29
4000–4999	6.52	2032.46	10.67	2072.52
5000–5999	7.31	2834.37	8.95	1831.76
6000–7999	12.79	2727.81	11.65	2355.41
8000–9999	6.75	1204.90	10.21	1964.85
10,000–14,999	8.38	1789.67	9.41	2935.56
15,000 or more	7.47	3059.70	14.57	2698.70
All families	10.59	2041.93	10.59	2041.93

TABLE D.4
Distribution of Veterans' Benefits

Dollar Values	By Current Income		By Economic Welfare Measure	
	Percentage Receiving Benefits	Average Benefit per Recipient Family	Percentage Receiving Benefits	Average Benefit per Recipient Family
Negative	3.14%	$1860.26	0 ¹%	$ 0
$ 0	16.69	807.37	—	—
1–499	13.86	901.87	2.80	1270.23
500–999	15.73	1117.16	2.26	985.45
1000–1499	9.99	862.65	7.87	1017.51
1500–1999	10.36	883.23	7.40	975.04
2000–2499	12.96	852.27	7.68	778.15
2500–2999	12.47	986.76	11.67	854.84
3000–3999	6.81	875.34	11.88	831.17
4000–4999	6.14	970.60	9.81	997.78
5000–5999	2.78	631.70	10.23	805.42
6000–7999	3.56	653.35	11.00	1105.64
8000–9999	1.14	388.05	8.07	798.35
10,000–14,999	2.07	1442.79	4.94	865.24
15,000 or more	1.86	460.55	5.12	1002.48
All families	9.41	918.92	9.41	918.92

TABLE D.5
Distribution of Unemployment and Workmen's Compensation Benefits

	By Current Income		By Economic Welfare Measure	
Dollar Values	Percentage Receiving Benefits	Average Benefit per Recipient Family	Percentage Receiving Benefits	Average Benefit per Recipient Family
Negative	0 %	$ 0	0 %	$ 0
$ 0	5.39	98.39	—	—
1–499	2.12	304.49	0	0
500–999	3.66	207.52	0	0
1000–1499	3.24	272.97	.89	328.46
1500–1999	1.42	288.43	2.91	141.20
2000–2499	.93	264.64	3.09	382.31
2500–2999	.93	676.32	1.89	220.58
3000–3999	2.11	580.28	3.03	336.65
4000–4999	4.50	313.45	4.10	339.59
5000–5999	4.81	435.61	3.70	465.20
6000–7999	5.74	460.62	3.03	328.98
8000–9999	4.69	399.31	.68	91.84
10,000–14,999	5.68	307.85	1.40	653.28
15,000 or more	.12	177.50	3.76	507.50
All families	2.80	348.21	2.80	348.21

TABLE D.6
Distribution of Medicare Benefits

Dollar Values	Average Benefit per Recipient Family	
	Current Income	Economic Welfare Measure
Negative	$283.07	$213.11
$ 0	224.07	—
1–499	228.50	229.60
500–999	206.89	209.48
1000–1499	216.27	204.22
1500–1999	231.37	214.19
2000–2499	231.22	216.39
2500–2999	241.12	232.92
3000–3999	244.33	238.55
4000–4999	252.45	241.35
5000–5999	287.22	253.05
6000–7999	263.67	276.19
8000–9999	274.46	307.99
10,000–14,999	347.55	305.89
15,000 or more	550.98	348.35
All families	247.17	247.17

TABLE D.7
Distribution of Medicaid Benefits

	By Current Income		By Economic Welfare Measure	
Dollar Values	Percentage Receiving Benefits	Average Benefit per Recipient Family	Percentage Receiving Benefits	Average Benefit per Recipient Family
Negative	18.75%	$242.88	82.14%	$228.71
$ 0	87.96	268.37	—	—
1–499	80.92	308.58	94.95	267.30
500–999	84.18	278.96	91.45	275.14
1000–1499	70.24	317.54	79.58	311.68
1500–1999	59.00	371.05	75.47	319.19
2000–2499	30.76	449.25	65.22	358.96
2500–2999	23.75	439.37	49.57	392.27
3000–3999	6.90	464.68	29.90	371.38
4000–4999	1.02	922.29	13.44	357.29
5000–5999	.57	306.52	12.30	383.11
6000–7999	.91	763.26	5.62	325.75
8000–9999	2.33	621.30	6.01	347.12
10,000–14,999	.08	613.38	2.92	339.76
15,000 or more	0	0	.10	142.70
All families	31.58	346.04	33.58	343.81

TABLE D.8

Distribution of Public Housing Benefits

Dollar Values	By Current Income		By Economic Welfare Measure	
	Percentage Receiving Benefits	Average Benefit per Recipient Family	Percentage Receiving Benefits	Average Benefit per Recipient Family
Negative	0 %	$ 0	0 %	$ 0
$ 0	3.27	504.60	—	—
1–499	1.14	104.37	15.80	751.89
500–999	2.98	441.75	2.70	332.40
1000–1499	2.21	465.43	6.93	408.80
1500–1999	2.13	320.87	3.02	428.35
2000–2499	1.59	403.10	2.35	346.45
2500–2999	.36	257.83	2.37	349.98
3000–3999	.37	228.73	.56	325.48
4000–4999	.42	256.79	.33	285.43
5000–5999	.20	260.80	.05	399.00
6000–7999	.08	87.00	0	0
8000–9999	.15	75.00	.59	87.00
10,000–14,999	0	0	0	0
15,000 or more	1.59	87.00	.15	156.27
All families	1.28	378.13	1.28	378.13

TABLE D.9
Distribution of Benefits from Double Personal Exemption

Dollar Values	By Current Income		By Economic Welfare Measure	
	Percentage Receiving Benefits	Average Benefit per Recipient Family	Percentage Receiving Benefits	Average Benefit per Recipient Family
Negative	0 %	$ 0	18.15%	$ 57.63
$ 0	0	0	—	—
1–499	0	0	1.28	72.67
500–999	0	0	.24	10.50
1000–1499	.84	27.74	10.58	138.39
1500–1999	1.11	57.57	10.59	142.12
2000–2499	6.47	52.22	7.90	125.86
2500–2999	14.70	46.19	15.21	95.80
3000–3999	37.62	71.31	18.57	128.09
4000–4999	67.90	122.75	30.27	102.39
5000–5999	78.69	140.25	42.62	124.66
6000–7999	81.20	142.31	44.59	139.58
8000–9999	93.91	158.54	50.28	142.20
10,000–14,999	96.73	175.00	57.89	143.03
15,000 or more	95.10	250.00	74.62	157.51
All families	28.37	130.64	28.37	130.64

TABLE D.10

Distribution of Benefits from Exclusion of Transfer Payments from Taxable Income

Dollar Values	By Current Income		By Economic Welfare Measure	
	Percentage Receiving Benefits	Average Benefit per Recipient Family	Percentage Receiving Benefits	Average Benefit per Recipient Family
Negative	0 %	$ 0	18.15%	$216.16
$ 0	0	0	—	—
1–499	0	0	13.67	144.19
500–999	0	0	.63	54.68
1000–1499	0	0	7.99	113.04
1500–1999	8.62	7.78	10.43	125.22
2000–2499	38.12	40.82	9.43	56.73
2500–2999	58.69	79.00	23.33	86.68
3000–3999	78.89	124.26	40.64	113.94
4000–4999	81.98	207.02	55.45	139.48
5000–5999	81.51	280.25	57.59	218.56
6000–7999	76.74	280.58	57.19	211.38
8000–9999	65.71	331.41	67.25	256.30
10,000–14,999	72.60	381.46	67.74	299.11
15,000 or more	50.95	752.10	72.92	378.74
All families	40.63	190.70	40.63	190.70

TABLE D.11
Distribution of Benefits from Retirement Income Tax Credit

Dollar Values	By Current Income		By Economic Welfare Measure	
	Percentage Receiving Benefits	Average Benefit per Recipient Family	Percentage Receiving Benefits	Average Benefit per Recipient Family
Negative	0 %	$ 0	1.48%	$235.04
$ 0	0	0	—	—
1–499	0	0	0	0
500–999	0	0	1.95	17.08
1000–1499	0	0	.80	106.56
1500–1999	0	0	1.25	125.18
2000–2499	1.48	58.71	.77	32.57
2500–2999	4.05	57.75	1.85	43.00
3000–3999	9.10	73.45	2.88	73.72
4000–4999	16.15	114.57	7.45	117.33
5000–5999	31.89	123.77	9.37	116.15
6000–7999	28.91	175.46	15.93	131.00
8000–9999	33.07	216.40	24.70	170.58
10,000–14,999	35.17	267.67	32.57	206.25
15,000 or more	36.89	302.64	36.63	258.14
All families	8.94	162.80	8.94	162.80

References

Aaron, H. 1972. *Shelters and subsidies*. Washington, D.C.: The Brookings Institution.

Ando, A., and Modigliani, F. 1963. The "life cycle" hypothesis of saving: aggregate implications and tests. *American Economic Review* 53:55–84.

Atkinson, A. B. 1970. On the measurement of inequality. *Journal of Economic Theory* 2: 244–63.

Baerwaldt, N., and Morgan, J. 1973. Trends in inter-family transfers. In L. Mandell et al., *Surveys of consumers* 1971–72. Ann Arbor, Mich.: Institute for Social Research.

Becker, G. 1965. A theory of the allocation of time. *Economic Journal* 75:493–517.

Bishop, G. 1967. *Tax burdens and benefits of government expenditures by income class, 1961 and 1965*. Tax Foundation, Research Publication no. 9. New York: Tax Foundation.

Bixby, L. 1970. Income of people aged 65 and older: overview from 1968 Survey of the Aged. *Social Security Bulletin* 33 (Apr. 1970): 3–34.

Bixby, L. et al. 1975. *Demographic and economic characteristics of the aged, 1968 Social Security Survey*. U.S. Dept. of Health, Education and Welfare, Social Security Administration, Office of Research and Statistics Research Report no. 45. Washington, D.C.: U.S. Government Printing Office.

Bridges, B., Jr. 1967. Current redistributional effects of old-age income assurance programs. In *Old-aged income assurance, Part 2*. U.S., Congress, Joint Economic Committee. Washington, D. C.: U.S. Government Printing Office.

Bridges, B., Jr. 1970. *Redistributive effects of transfer payments among age and economic status groups*. U.S. Dept. of Health, Education and Welfare. Social Security Administration Staff Paper no. 10. Washington, D.C.: U.S. Government Printing Office.

Brittain, J. 1971. The incidence of Social Security payroll taxes. *American Economic Review* 61 (Mar. 1971):110–25.

Brittain, J. 1972. The incidence of the Social Security payroll tax: reply *American Economic Review* 62 (Sept. 1972):739–42.

Chen, Y.-P. 1967. Potential income from homeownership: an actuarial mortgage plan. In *Old age income assurance, Part 2*. U.S. Congress Joint Economic Committee. Washington, D.C.: U.S. Government Printing Office.

Chen, Y.-P. 1971. *Income: background and issues*. White House Conference on Aging. Washington, D.C.: Government Printing Office.

Commerce Clearing House. 1968. *Complete guide to Medicare.* New York: Commerce Clearing House.

Cooper, B. S., and Piro, P. A. 1974. Age differences in medical care spending, fiscal year 1973. *Social Security Bulletin* 37 (May 1974):3–14.

David, M. 1959. Welfare, income, and budget needs. *Review of Economics and Statistics* 41 (Nov. 1959):393–99.

Davis, K., and Reynolds, R. 1973. Medicare and the utilization of health care services by the elderly. Mimeographed. Washington, D.C.: The Brookings Institution.

Epstein, L., and Murray, J. 1967. *The aged population of the United States—the 1963 Social Security Survey of the Aged.* U.S. Dept. of Health, Education, and Welfare, Social Security Administration. Washington, D.C.: U.S. Government Printing Office.

Feldstein, M. S. 1971. An econometric model of the Medicare system. *Quarterly Journal of Economics* 85 (Feb. 1971):1–20.

Feldstein, M. S. 1972. The incidence of the Social Security payroll tax: comment. *American Economic Review* 62 (Sept. 1972):735–38.

Gallaway, L. 1965. *The retirement decision.* U.S. Dept. of Health, Education, and Welfare, Social Security Administration Research Report no. 9. Washington, D.C.: U.S. Government Printing Office.

Garfinkel, I., and Kesselman, J. 1976. On the efficiency of income testing in tax-transfer programs. Mimeographed.

Gillespie, W. I. 1965. Effect of public expenditures on the distribution of income. In *Essays in fiscal federalism,* ed. R. A. Musgrave, pp. 122–86. Washington, D.C.: The Brookings Institution.

Hall, R. E. 1973. Wages, income and hours of work in the U.S. labor force. In *Income maintenance and labor supply,* ed. G. Cain and H. Watts, pp. 102–62. Chicago: Markham Press.

Henderson, J., and Quandt, R. 1958. *Microeconomic theory.* New York: McGraw-Hill.

Holahan, J. 1975. *Financing health care for the poor.* Lexington, Mass.: Lexington Books.

Joseph, M. F. W. 1939. The excess burden of indirect taxation. *Review of Economic Studies* 21 (June 1939):226–31.

Kreps, J. 1971. *Lifetime allocation of work and income.* Durham, N.C.: Duke University Press.

Little, I. M. D. 1951. Direct vs. indirect taxes. *Economic Journal* 61 (Sept. 1951):557–84.

Moon, M. L. 1976. The economic welfare of the aged and income security programs. *Review of Income and Wealth* 22 (Sept. 1976):253–69.

Morgan, J. 1968. The supply of effort, the measurement of wellbeing and the dynamics of improvement. *American Economic Review* 58 (May 1968): 31–39.

Morgan, J. et al. 1962. *Income and welfare in the United States.* New York: McGraw-Hill.

Murray, J. 1971. Living arrangements of people aged 65 and older: findings from the 1968 Survey of the Aged. *Social Security Bulletin* 34 (Sept. 1971):3–14.

Murray, J. 1972. Homeownership and financial assets: findings from the 1968 Survey of the Aged. *Social Security Bulletin* 35 (Aug. 1972):6–15.

O'Connor, J. 1971. The redistributive effects of Title XIX of the Social Security Act: a statistical study for 1968. Ph.D. dissertation, University of Notre Dame.

Orshansky, M. 1968. The shape of poverty in 1966. *Social Security Bulletin* 31 (Mar. 1968):3–31.

Pechman, J. 1971. *Federal tax policy.* New York: W. W. Norton.

Pechman, J.; Aaron, H.; and Taussig, M. 1968. *Social Security perspectives for reform.* Washington, D.C.: The Brookings Institution.

Pechman, J., and Okner. B. 1974. *Who bears the tax burden?* Washington, D.C.: The Brookings Institution.

Projector, D., and Weiss, G. 1966. *Survey of financial characteristics of consumers.* Board of Governors of the Federal Reserve System. Washington, D.C.: Government Printing Office.

Projector, D., and Weiss, G. 1969. Income–net worth measures of economic welfare. *Social Security Bulletin* 32 (Nov. 1969):14–17.

Reynolds, M., and Smolensky, E. 1974. The post fisc distribution: 1961 and 1970 compared. *National Tax Journal* 27 (Dec. 1974):515–30.

Schmundt, M.; Smolensky, E.; and Stiefel, L. 1975. The evaluation by recipients of in-kind transfers. In *Integrating income maintenance programs,* ed. I. Lurie, pp. 189–207. New York: Academic Press.

Schultze, C. L. et al. 1972. *Setting national priorities; the 1973 budget.* Washington, D.C.: The Brookings Institution.

Sirageldin, I. 1969. *Non-market components of national income.* Ann Arbor: Survey Research Center, University of Michigan.

Skolnik, A. M., and Dales, S. R. 1975. Social welfare expenditures, fiscal year 1974. *Social Security Bulletin* 38 (Jan. 1975):3–19.

Smolensky, E., and Gomery, J. D. 1973. Efficiency and equity effects in the benefits from the Federal Housing Program in 1965. In *Benefit–cost analyses of federal programs,* U.S. Congress Joint Economic Committee, pp. 144–81. Washington, D.C.: U.S. Government Printing Office.

Steiner, P., and Dorfman, R. 1957. *The economic status of the aged,* pp. 82–92. Berkeley: University of California Press.

Stuart, B. 1971. *Health care and income.* Michigan, Dept. of Health Services Research Report no. 5. Lansing: State of Michigan.

Surrey, S., and Hellmuth, W. 1969. The tax expenditure budget. *National Tax Journal* 22 (Dec. 1969):528–30.

Taussig, M. 1973. *Alternative measures of the distribution of economic welfare.* Princeton, N.J.: Industrial Relations Section, Princeton University.

U.S., Bureau of the Budget. 1972. Special analyses of the budget for fiscal year 1973. Washington, D.C.: Government Printing Office.

U.S., Bureau of the Census. 1970. *Statistical abstract of the U.S., 1970.* 91st ed. Washington, D.C.: U.S. Government Printing Office.

U.S., Bureau of the Census. 1973. Current population reports, Series P–60, no. 91, *Characteristics of the low income population, 1972.* Washington, D.C.: U.S. Government Printing Office.

U.S., Dept. of Health, Education and Welfare. [1967]. *Recipients and amounts of medical vendor payments under public assistance programs, January–June 1967.* National Center for Social Statistics Report B-3. Washington, D.C.: U.S. Government Printing Office.

U.S., Dept. of Health, Education and Welfare. 1967. *Recipients and amounts of medical vendor payments under public assistance programs, July 1966–December 1967.* National Center for Social Statistics Report B-3. Washington, D.C.: U.S. Government Printing Office.

U.S., Dept. of Health, Education and Welfare. 1972. *Number of recipients and amounts of payments under Medicaid and other medical programs financed from public assistance funds, 1969.* National Center for Social Statistics Report B-4. Washington, D.C.: U.S. Government Printing Office.

U.S., Dept. of Labor, Bureau of Labor Statistics. 1974. *Handbook of labor statistics 1974*. Washington, D.C.: U.S. Government Printing Office.

U.S., Public Health Service. 1971. *Vital statistics of the United States*, vol. 2, 1967, Part A, Mortality. Washington, D.C.: U.S. Government Printing Office.

Watts, H. 1969. An economic definition of poverty. In *On understanding poverty*, ed. D. P. Moynihan, pp. 316–329. New York: Basic Books.

Weisbrod, B. 1970. Collective action and the distribution of income: a conceptual approach. In *Public expenditures and policy analysis*, ed. R. Haveman and J. Margolis, pp. 117–40. Chicago: Markham.

Weisbrod, B. A., and Hansen, W. L. 1968. An income–net worth approach to measuring economic welfare. *American Economic Review* 58 (Dec. 1968):1315–29.

Wisconsin, Dept. of Health and Social Services, Division on Aging. 1971. *The needs of Wisconsin's older people*, vol. 2. Madison.

Subject Index

A
B
C
D
E
F
G
H
I
J